UNEMPLOYABLE!

HOW TO BE SUCCESSFULLY UNEMPLOYED YOUR ENTIRE LIFE

David Thomas Roberts

Unemployable!

ISBN 13: 978-0-9962590-1-9 hardback
ISBN 13: 978-0-9962590-4-0 paperback
ISBN 13: 978-0-9962590-5-7 digital-epub
ISBN 13: 978-0-9962590-6-4 digital-mobi

Published in The Republic of Texas

Disclaimer – Neither the author nor any other person(s) associated with this book may be held liable for any damages that may result from any of the ideas or recommendations made by the author in this book. No single book of financial advice or starting a business can be used as a substitute for professional advice. Readers are strongly encouraged to seek professional advice from qualified financial advisors, attorneys and accountants before embarking on any of the ideas in this book. Under no circumstances will any legal responsibility or blame be held against the publisher or author for any reparation, damages, or monetary loss due to the information contained herein, either directly or indirectly.

For more bestselling titles below by David Thomas Roberts visit www.defiancepress.com or Amazon.

A State of Treason
Patriots of Treason

David Thomas Roberts is an accomplished speaker and is available for public or private speaking events on both business and politics. Please contact Defiance Press & Publishing at 1-888-315-9446 for more information.

Bulk order quotes of this book may be obtained by contacting Defiance Press & Publishing at www.defiancepress.com or 1-888-315-9446.

Printed in USA

Dedication

This book is dedicated to my four children –Tiffany, Tanya, Travis and Tanner. They inspired and encouraged me to write this book and have been first-hand witnesses (and many times participants) to the philosophies, struggles and the successes documented in the following pages. I pray that they are able to take my experiences and use them to follow their own unique path to their individual definitions of success!

TABLE OF CONTENTS

FOREWORD

The ideas for this book are based on my experiences, both successes and failures, in over thirty years of being self-employed. I sincerely hope the experiences, ideas and somewhat unique philosophies that have guided me are of some benefit to you in your quest for your own definition of success.

What separates this book from the thousands of "how-to" titles available on entrepreneurship and how to start a business?

I've done it.

I've failed.

I've succeeded.

This book is not about *theory*. My classroom and professors have been my real-life experiences in starting and running businesses of many kinds.

I've gone broke — twice.

I've learned from the mistakes I made that led to those failures.

I've never quit trying — *ever*.

For years now, my wife and I have been in the top 1/10th of 1 percent of incomes in America. We have reached a seven-figure net worth. We have money in the bank, no serious debt, an incredible home and lots of toys.

We have been able to contribute to the charities of our choice and the political candidates we believe in. We have been able to help our children when necessary.

We have peace of mind.

I learned long ago to listen to some sage advice: *"Find someone who has what you want or has done what you want to do and do what they did."*

This book is especially for those who, like me, believe having a job and sitting in a cubicle every day is akin to slow and painful torture.

If you have a burning desire to be your own boss and make your own mark in the world, read on.

If you walk into a business and immediately start trying to reverse-engineer it, its gross revenue and profit, read on.

If successful people fascinate you and you look for any opportunity to pick their brains, read on.

If you go to work every day miserable, read on.

If you're tired of living paycheck to paycheck, read on.

If you hate your boss, read on.

If you're willing to eat beans for now to eat steak every day later, read on.

If you have a great idea for a business or invention, read on.

If you absolutely know you *have* to be in business for yourself, yet you don't know what to do, read on.

Are entrepreneurs *made* or *born*? Read on!

"It doesn't matter how many times you fail. It doesn't matter how many times you almost get it right. No one is going to know or care about your failures, and neither should you. All you have to do is learn from them and those around you because all that matters in business is that you get it right once. Then everyone can tell you how lucky you are."

—Mark Cuban
Billionaire owner of the Dallas Mavericks
Co-founder of Broadcast.com
Founder of HDNet

CHAPTER 1

YOU CAN'T PUSH A WET NOODLE

"Is this the life I dreamed of — or is this just the way it all went down?"

—*Pat Green*
Texas Music Legend
Grammy Nominated Recording Artist
Lyrics from the song "California"

I magine twenty years from now asking yourself that question.

How do you predict you will answer it?

Some people resign themselves to whatever fate they believe they have been chained to.

Were you born to wake up every morning, then climb into your car, and fight commuter traffic, only to report to a job you likely hate? Can you imagine doing the same thing for the next five, ten or twenty years?

Have you ever driven to your job and, after arriving, find that you actually forgot the details of the commute?

"Did I stop at that signal? Was it red or green?"

Try it sometime. Think about your last commute. Can you remember *any* details of the drive? It's almost like your car *automatically* knows where to go every day.

Yet this is accepted behavior by the masses. This commuting in traffic is part of the plan. Aren't we all taught to get a good *job*? It's normal accepted behavior that a good job involves a morning and late afternoon commute.

What exactly is a *good* job?

John is a corporate executive living in the suburbs. He would love to live closer to his job, but the housing costs nearer to his downtown employer are just too expensive. Besides, he wants his kids to grow up in a certain school district and his wife Jane wants to live the suburbia lifestyle. Jane has a job of her own, but hers is only a thirty-minute drive away in traffic after she drops off the two kids at day care.

John's twenty-eight mile commute takes about forty-five minutes in the morning and closer to an hour in the afternoon — but only if he leaves by a certain time from his house and from his office. If he leaves at the wrong time, each segment of his commute takes more than an hour. It takes John about an hour each day to recover from the rude drivers, stress and monotony of the drive.

John just got a new boss. Instead of promoting from within, his company brought in this new guy and, unbelievably, he was brought in from an entirely different industry. John's new boss seeks him out often for tidbits on how to do *his* job.

John changed jobs almost two years ago to make $11,000 more in annual salary. His new job provides one week less vacation until he hits his two-year anniversary, but he thinks the trade-off for more money is worth it. The benefits are about the same, even though the drive is fifteen miles longer on a much more congested route.

Kathy is a dynamic sales professional just completing her most successful year ever for a company she has worked at for more than six years. Her bonus commissions put her at a higher income than her sales manager for the first time ever. Having none of that, the sales manager changed the commission plan and made it immediately *retroactive*, effectively eliminating the bonus she had already earned. The newly revised commission plan will require Kathy to produce thirty percent more business just to keep pace with what she made the year before. Her dream of an exotic family vacation with the bonus commissions she thought she had earned will have to wait.

Kathy thought about quitting on the spot with the commission change, but uncertainty made her hesitate. She is actively looking for a new job while still employed at her current position; however, she will have to change industries because she signed a non-compete agreement with her current employer.

Mickey, an IT professional for a large publicly traded company, has saved his company millions of dollars in efficiency costs, improved processes and streamlined technology implementations. At his annual review, his division manager gave him the highest marks available, yet he only received a three percent cost-of-living increase.

Quiet and reserved by nature, Mickey continually sees others in his company, including his boss, take credit for his ideas and improvements. During small talk with his boss after the review, he learns his boss just bought a large new home in an exclusive area of town. Scuttlebutt at the office says the regional manager received a large bonus based on the budget savings Mickey's ideas delivered to the company.

Marcia gets up at 5:00 a.m. every morning to get herself and her two small children dressed and fed, then drops them off at day care in order to be at work by 7:00 a.m. Her husband Bill rides a van pool, which picks him up in front of his house at 7:15 a.m. to get to work every day.

With one toddler only eighteen months old, the second child was a surprise. The couple decided to sell one of their cars to get rid of a large car note, insurance, fuel and maintenance expenses so they could afford the cost of day care. Bill is not crazy about the van pool nor the occupants he shares the van with, but "you have to do what you have to do," he reasons to himself.

What Bill and Marcia haven't figured out is that, by the time they pay for day care, business clothes, lunches, commuting expenses and the extra taxes from the more punitive tax bracket Marcia's salary puts them in, they are actually *losing* money by Marcia working! And they may never figure this out because they don't really know how to adequately measure their decisions from a financial perspective.

These stories are just a few examples of the millions like this that repeat themselves every day in America.

My question is, *why?*

Isn't the very definition of *insanity* to keep doing the same thing over and over and expecting different results?

Some folks love their jobs. That's great! Entrepreneurship is not for all people. As you launch out on your own and build your business, it's very possible you will need motivated and dedicated employees. You and I should be glad the employee pool is large and always will be.

Make no mistake; anyone can be a success in his or her own business, but not everyone wants to be, or believes it is possible. I'll never understand that fully, but it is what it is.

Entrepreneurs tend to be blind to obstacles. It doesn't mean we don't see them or acknowledge their existence; we just don't let obstacles determine our success or failure.

Failure is never permanent; it's only a temporary obstacle to overcome. I don't know a single successful entrepreneur who hasn't experienced failures.

So why do people readily accept the real-life scenarios pictured in this chapter?

One of the many things in life I have learned is that I can't motivate others if they are not already motivated on their own. I can give them tools, direction and resources, but I can't motivate them — and I can't create a strong work ethic in them. It has to be there already.

You can't push a wet noodle…

For those like me, the *fear* of living life like those examples is more powerful than the lure of making millions of dollars.

So *what* exactly motivates you?

Are you tired of being broke and living paycheck to paycheck?

Are you sick and tired of being sick and tired?

Does the sheer thought of doing what you currently do to make a living for the next five, ten or twenty years stir you into a near panic attack?

Are you bothered that somebody dictates your daily schedule, how much you make, when you can take a vacation and where you live?

Do you dream of being in business for yourself?

Are you constantly trying to figure out what business to start?

Congratulations!

You are probably *unemployable*, too!

Lessons Learned:

▶ *Business ownership is not for everyone, and that's okay.*

▶ *There are many different forms of motivation. Figure out what motivates you.*

▶ *Don't accept society's norms for what you are supposed to do with your life.*

CHAPTER 2

THE *RENEGADE CAPITALIST*® AND THE GIG ECONOMY

"Most important: merge your passion and skill with something that is useful to other people."

—Chris Guillebeau, Entrepreneur
Author of "The $100 Startup"

M illennials (those 18-35 years old at the writing of this book) have learned to question all the norms. This generation is the most connected and unconventional generation in history. Millennials have grasped the emergence of new technologies with a voracious appetite. The rest of us have had to come along for the ride.

More and more, we are seeing the emergence of the *Gig Economy*. Many millennials, like all entrepreneurs, openly question the status quo and why certain behaviors for business, life and society are the way they are.

What is the *Gig Economy*?

Essentially, it's the proliferation of a new generation of *Micro Businesses*.

Micro businesses have been around from the beginning of time.

These include the world's oldest profession to the family selling loaves of bread or fruits and vegetables on a cobblestone street in Roman times.

What is different today is the technology, information and unparalleled connectivity that allows micro businesses to sell products, services and information worldwide. No longer are businesses tied to a single location, storefront, inventory or local customer base.

The speed at which a micro business can be launched is unprecedented and is limited only by one's imagination.

It is the freedom to be unshackled from conventional norms of business, such as reporting to a store or office and keeping eight-to-five hours, or conducting business from wherever *you* decide.

I have dubbed those entrepreneurs that have capitalized on the Gig Economy as *Renegade Capitalists®.*

Who says you have to be at work by eight a.m.? Who says you have to work until five p.m.? Who says you can't work from wherever you can connect to the Internet or your email? Who says you have to live close to your customers, or that you can't have a global business from your home?

Cynthia is a personal trainer living in a large metropolitan area. She typically has clients four days a week in the early morning hours. In the afternoons, she takes on freelance graphic design jobs she bids on through multiple freelance graphic design sites designed to match designers with those who need business cards, websites, company logos, and presentations.

Cynthia never went to school to learn graphic design; she taught herself how to use an off-the-shelf software application in a matter of days. Her average profit per job is $400 and she averages 2-3 per week.

After doing some design work for several covers for self-published authors, she decided to put some of her successful physical training techniques into an e-book and sell it on Amazon. She has created such a following that she publishes a new e-book about every sixty days. Cynthia created a nice residual income from ebook sales, and now maintains a blog on which various health and nutrition providers buy advertising.

Cynthia makes enough money to give up the daily private physical training clients she has but, because she genuinely cares about her small base of clients and because it is truly a passion she loves, she elects to continue the training. *She does it because she wants to, not because she has to*. Her other income streams don't require her to be at a specific location or report anywhere at a certain time. Cynthia is a *Renegade Capitalist®*.

A *Renegade Capitalist®* is an individual who rejects conventional behavior, especially when it comes to the social and business norms associated with running or owning a business.

A *Renegade Capitalist®* applies his or her unconventional ideas to *capitalism*, an economic system in which investment in and ownership of the means of production, distribution, and exchange of wealth is made and maintained chiefly by private individuals or corporations instead of government-owned means of wealth.

No matter your age, you can take advantage of some of the most dynamic forces that have ever occurred in the history of business.

Kyle is twenty-six, single and a freelance photographer. He always knew his interest was in photography and took classes in community college after high school. Traveling anywhere in the world he wants to, Kyle snaps professional photographs that he posts to his website for sale to designers, artists or anyone who enjoys his photos. He has regular clients who order photographs from him to use in their own publications.

Need a picture of the Taj Mahal at sunrise? How about a cheetah in the Serengeti Desert at sundown or an Alaskan Kodiak brown bear on Kodiak Island in the rain? Kyle's your guy! He lists his upcoming travel plans on his website so you can request specific photos for a price. Kyle's inventory of pictures is huge. He sells many of his pictures to stock photo websites who pay him a royalty every time someone downloads one of his pictures.

Kyle's signature trademarks are his black-and-white photographs of very remote places, people, landscapes, architecture and animals.

Kyle's blog details his worldly travels. He learned the value of residual income by having some of his customers pay him on retainer, so he has a steady income stream while he travels and until he sells his next collage of Himalayan mountainscapes!

All Kyle needs to operate a business are his laptop, photography equipment, and connectivity to upload his latest pictures to his site, to send to waiting clients, or to the Cloud for use or sale later. When Kyle is remote, he simply logs in and uploads the images when he eventually has connectivity.

Knowing the power of social media, Kyle updates his Twitter, Instagram and Facebook pages with his images to create a very large following of fans when he is not too remote and has Internet connectivity.

All his customer transactions are paid with PayPal or credit card, which go straight to his bank account, and he uses a debit card for cash while on his travels. He is completely free of an office or phone. His customers know any email they send him may take a couple of weeks to get answered. He doesn't own a home or a car, nor does he feel pressured by society to own either.

Kyle took a traditional business (photography studio) and applied *Renegade Capitalist®* fundamentals to create an incredible amount of freedom while pursuing his passion.

Jim and Nancy joined a network marketing company to supplement the income they got from their corporate jobs. By promoting the products and services of the network marketing company to friends, family and business associates, they were able to replace Nancy's income within eight months. The couple earns a royalty on all downline distributors' sales, and their distribution organization has grown to thousands, allowing Jim to also leave his corporate management job. They both work from home offices in their new 10,000 square-foot home.

Jim and Nancy have learned the power of duplication and residual income (discussed in detail in later chapters) and now do most of their business through web meetings and conference calls.

Marty was working 70+ hours per week as a trial lawyer, but her passion was her dogs. Like many people who love their pets, her male and female boxers were part of the family.

Marty wanted to get a portrait commissioned for a watercolor painting of her two beloved pets. Unable to find a local artist, Marty went online but still couldn't find a suitable artist who didn't need the dogs to "sit" for the drawing, which would require her to travel hundreds of miles with the dogs.

In talking to other pet owners (*ah... marketing research!),* Marty discovered that many others would like to have a painting, drawing, sketch or watercolor of their family pets. The idea for a business was born!

Marty had her husband make a video, and she posted the video and the project on a crowdfunding site. The money she raised was to be used for the website, marketing, and to attract freelance artists of all kinds. Her goal was to raise $10,000 in increments of $25 or more. If someone donated $100 or more, they got a sketch of their pet, all the way to $1,000, which earned the crowdfunding contributor an original oil painting. All they had to do was to upload a few photos of their beloved feline, canine or other pet.

To her astonishment, she raised $25,000 without giving up any equity in the newly funded company, and she was off and running. Marty got the website, artists and process down to a science. Clients upload images to the site and, depending on the request, are re-routed to the appropriate artists who produce the drawing or painting, which is then drop-shipped to the customer. Marty never has to touch the drawings or handle the shipping. Many of her artists now make a full-time living on the production of these pet masterpieces.

Customers can post reviews of the artists as they compete for the highest ratings and customer satisfaction. Customers are guaranteed 100 percent satisfaction and can return the finished product and transfer the project to a new artist.

Marty facilitates the collection of fees from the customer, paid online before the project begins, and then she pays the artists after the customer receives the artwork. Now she is expanding into other areas of art production from pictures for sports, children and architecture.

Marty left the legal world and the 70+ hours a week behind forever. Like other *Renegade Capitalists®*, she has leveraged the technology that produces self-generating marketing, collection and customer service to provide her with the freedom so many covet yet never attain.

Lessons Learned:

▶ *Today's entrepreneur has unprecedented opportunities to quickly launch a business idea.*

▶ *Those who figure out the Gig Economy can design a business with unlimited potential and personal freedom.*

▶ *A Renegade Capitalist® challenges the norms of traditional business models to fit his or her definition of what makes any particular business a success.*

▶ *A micro business is relatively easy to start — you just need an idea and the willingness to take action!*

CHAPTER 3

WHY NOT ME?

"What separates the successful entrepreneurs from the non-successful ones is pure perseverance."

—Steve Jobs
Entrepreneur and Co-Founder of Apple

From the earliest age I can remember, we were told that we were all created equal. If that was true, why did it seem some families had larger homes, fancier cars, nicer clothes, whose kids attended better schools, took great vacations, and appeared not to have to worry about money?

Was it luck?

Did they have some inherent advantages I didn't have?

Were they smarter than me?

Did they know the right people?

Did they come from the right families?

Did they already have money?

Notwithstanding the obvious material possessions, why did they seem to have a higher quality of life?

How was someone able to give so much to his or her church?

I was always fascinated by the differences apparent to me in the lifestyles and ultimately the happiness of those who were in business for themselves versus those who simply had a job.

Let me state unequivocally that I am not against anyone's chosen profession. There are many important jobs to fill and many people find their own happiness working for someone else. We absolutely need to have people fill the roles of policemen, firemen, clergy, career military, accountants, bank tellers, scientists, janitors, teachers, nurses, plumbers and mechanics.

Some people grow up trying to figure out how things are put together and how they work. Today, a young person may be intrigued with how gaming software works or how a smartphone application is developed. In my younger days, if you were so inclined, you might have built a go-kart from a lawnmower engine or rebuilt a dilapidated car so you could have your first set of wheels.

For me, I was always curious how it was that people lived in the huge homes not far from our neighborhood. But I also asked why people lived in tenements and slums. Was it a case of luck? Was it genetics? Were poor people just unlucky? When I went to downtown Houston with my parents, I wondered who owned the huge skyscrapers, and how someone could afford to build them. Yet, if you traveled not too many blocks away from those gleaming glass towers, you could find abject poverty.

Why did my best friends' parents seem to have more free time to spend with their kids? Why did they get to go on skiing vacations and have a boat while we went on vacations to relatives' homes or just stayed home? Why did there always seem to be a high degree of tension in our family caused by financial stress?

I will be the first person to agree that success is not measured by the size of your home, how fancy your car is, or how much money you have in the bank. There are plenty of people in life with lots of money and financial success whose lives are disasters and who are miserable, even by their own accounts.

Success for me is the freedom to do the things I love without others controlling my time, income or schedule, and without worrying about money.

Misery for me would be being "employed" by the standard most of us are taught to follow as we go through the educational system. I completely understand that there are those in life who find fulfilling careers and happiness in whatever they do, including being employees for large corporations their entire lives. They are completely at ease with an employer who determines their schedules, pay, benefits, length of vacations, and promotions. I have some great employees in my businesses. This book is not intended to be critical of those who choose this path for their careers and lives.

On the other hand, if the thought of working the next forty years as an employee literally terrifies you and you really want to know what separates entrepreneurs and business owners from an employee mentality and, if you simply burn for the opportunity to be in business for yourself, this book is for you.

Maybe you're just like I was — **"Unemployable!"**

Lessons Learned:

▶ *Everyone is created with an equal opportunity to become unequal.*

▶ *Study and learn what makes certain people successful.*

▶ *Ultimately make your own luck.*

▶ *What a shame it would be to go through life never experiencing "what we would have become."*

CHAPTER 4

DO YOU HAVE THE "DNA"?

"The critical ingredient is getting off your butt and doing something. It's as simple as that. A lot of people have ideas, but there are few who decide to do something about them now. Not tomorrow. Not next week. But today. The true entrepreneur is a doer, not a dreamer."

—Nolan Bushnell
Entrepreneur, Founder of Atari and Chuck E. Cheese

Many people think entrepreneurs are born and not made. What really makes business owners different? Do some people just have *it* — whatever *it* is? Are they immune to risk, gamblers at heart? Are they natural-born salespeople?

Do I need the formula for the next *Big Thing*? What if I don't have any money and live paycheck to paycheck?

Some people are natural renegades who don't like being controlled by a boss or schedule. I can attest that this is exactly the mentality of many entrepreneurs. If you have ever had the thought that you could "make something better," or "had a better idea," or bristled at the thought of someone you don't respect dictating to you from eight to five, then you are probably cut from the same cloth I am.

Not all of us were born with the desire to start our own businesses. For some, the decision may have come later in life after years of corporate employment for reasons stemming from layoffs and downsizing to finally deciding to pursue what they really love. For others, it could be another kind of motivation, such as health reasons. Some do it because they feel they are never paid what they are worth. Whatever the reason, the most common trait I have found in entrepreneurs is that streak of independent nature they are either born with or developed.

My parents didn't believe in allowances. I wasn't paid to do the chores I was assigned. If I wanted items or extra money, I would go to the neighbors and pull weeds from their flowerbeds, mow their lawns, or wash their cars to earn money. We even got permission to dive for golf balls at a local golf course, then sold the used balls in egg cartons. I got my first job pulling trap and skeet at a local firing range, and then sacked groceries at a food store.

I'm no psychologist, but I believe we are all born with a blank slate and, even though our personalities are somewhat pre-wired, our values and belief systems are impacted by environmental factors. How many times have you seen police officers choose their paths because their fathers and grandfathers were cops? How about coal miners who have worked in the mines for five generations?

Environmental factors can also produce negative motivation, like it did for me as I watched my stepfather toil in corporate America. I sometimes wonder if my defiant streak would still be there had I not seen how he was treated after thirty-five years of loyalty to this giant corporation.

For people like you and me, there is something that motivates us to choose this path and, from what I've seen, the factors that lead people to seek their own independence are as varied as there are people. But make no mistake: for serious entrepreneurs, their need for independence is as important as their next breath!

America was built on the self-reliance of entrepreneurs such as ranchers, farmers, shopkeepers, millers, blacksmiths, hoteliers, and others who may have had only their wits and their two hands to fashion some kind of independent lives from nothing.

Immigrants coming to the United States typically brought a trade with them and, because of their lack of education, capital and knowledge of English, simply began plying their trades when and where they could. In the late 1800s and through most of the early 1900s, America was a nation of small business owners.

Today our children are indoctrinated in our educational system to prepare for a "job" when their education at their desired level is complete. America has transformed from a free enterprise society to the general acceptance of life involving the prospect of holding down a job for most if not your entire life.

But, if you have a deep-down, gut-level instinct to forge your own path, there are still exciting opportunities in today's modern society to gain your freedom and financial independence. In fact, it can be argued that, despite an overreaching level of government regulations, government interference, taxes and red tape, this may be the best time in history to start your own business, especially with the advances in technology, medicine and information.

No matter what venture or idea you hope to make into a successful business, I have found there are tried and true attributes that are common for most successful entrepreneurs. There are also significant differences in business types.

What does it take to succeed in business for yourself?

Hard work. Dreams. Planning. Desire.

But, most important, it requires Action!

Lessons Learned:

► *Entrepreneurs are made, not born.*

► *Burning desire is the most common trait among entrepreneurs.*

► *Take action to follow your dreams now; don't wait.*

CHAPTER 5

WHAT REALLY IS AN ENTREPRENEUR?

"Instead of trying to make your life perfect, give yourself the freedom to make it an adventure..."

—Drew Houston
Founder of Dropbox
Billionaire Entrepreneur

A t a publishing conference recently, I heard a speaker describe an entrepreneur as *"Someone who brings value to an idea."* I couldn't have said it any simpler or better. I believe entrepreneurs have a special knack for identifying problems that can be solved by their unique solution.

I had a spirited discussion with an academic elite who was a PhD from a prestigious university in which he refused to classify a common business owner as an "entrepreneur." His argument was that only someone who had changed an industry or invented the next *Big Thing* fit his narrow definition of the term.

For me, an entrepreneur can be as common as a business owner who decides to open a dry cleaners on a corner that doesn't have one. Did he or she invent any intellectual property, or get a U.S. patent on a cleaning solution? No. He or she brought value to an idea that a dry cleaners on that corner would serve the community and would be successful, and they made it happen!

A couple of years ago, I spoke to the graduating MBA class at The University of Texas in Austin. They wanted to hear my story about the bootstrapping (low start-up investment) of Teligistics, our very successful technology company in the telecommunications industry.

To most of these students, the idea of starting a business with very little money was completely foreign to them. The typical MBA who has dreams of business ownership is busy putting together a massive business plan and is pitching the plan to private equity groups or venture capital firms. Most of these involve millions of dollars in start-up costs.

Although there are many examples of historically successfully startups who have gone this route, such as Facebook and others that were funded by large investments, the vast majority of businesses start small and typically with money that has been saved or borrowed. Some of the largest firms in the Fortune 500 today were started many years ago with an idea and very little money.

There are legions of well-financed bad ideas that are on the junk heap of business history.

Many entrepreneurs have taken proven ideas and simply improved them or given them additional value. Take the example of the dry cleaners. For my wife and me, one of the things we detested was dropping off and picking up our dry cleaning. For many with the hectic schedules of work, school, and children's activities, the grind of the dry cleaner drop-off and pick-up is a necessary pain.

My naturally inquisitive nature would often ask: Why couldn't dry cleaners offer a pick-up and delivery service in our suburban area? I knew there were commercial uniform services that delivered work uniforms to industry, hospitals and other businesses. Why couldn't someone offer this locally to residences?

When I asked local dry cleaners in the area this question, I was told there were too many variables. It would be too expensive. What if the homeowner wasn't home when dry cleaning was delivered? How does the dry cleaner collect money? Logistics was a nightmare. Excuse after excuse. Instead of these businesses listening to the needs of their customers, they basically dismissed my idea.

The best indicator to me that this was an opportunity waiting for someone to solve it is the fact my wife and I were willing to pay MORE for this service than we currently paid to have our clothes dry cleaned.

Before long, a company consolidated several small local dry cleaning stores and plants and began offering this "white glove" pick-up and delivery service, which we cheerfully subscribed to immediately.

This entrepreneur solved the obstacles of those who thought this idea was "impossible." First, the company keeps a credit card on file to charge customers automatically. Collection problem solved. Second, they pick up, every Monday, a cloth bag they supply with the service that we put outside our front door tagged with our information for pick up. The cleaning service then returns our dry cleaning to a hook outside a door away from any weather on Thursdays. Neither one of us has to be home. If they have a question about any of the garments, they call us.

This company brought value to the idea of the pick-up and

delivery of customer dry cleaning. They solved the problems their competitors could never figure out or never thought people like my wife and I would pay more for.

This business owner is every bit the entrepreneur, but the PhD could not wrap his brain around the fact he or she didn't get a venture capitalist involved or raise millions of dollars to launch the company.

History has shown many of the best ideas are simple ones. This small business took an unglamorous business and made it unique — and one my wife and I can't live without!

Lessons Learned:

- ▶ *Entrepreneurs bring value to ideas — even ideas that improve existing business models. They are not necessarily inventors of the "Next Big Thing."*
- ▶ *Entrepreneurs identify marketable solutions to problems.*
- ▶ *Entrepreneurs question EVERYTHING, including the norms of acceptable business models, constantly looking to improve on them with their own ideas.*

CHAPTER 6

THE COMPANY MAN

"(Retirement) is predicated on the assumption that you dislike what you are doing during the most physically capable years of your life. This is a non-starter — nothing can justify that sacrifice."

—Timothy Ferris
Serial Entrepreneur
Author of "The 4-Hour Workweek"

I'll never forget walking into our new house in Houston when my stepfather was transferred from San Antonio to Houston in 1969. The house had just been built and the entire family was excited to be moving into a much larger new home.

When we walked into the house the first time, I was amazed at how large it seemed with its plush avocado green shag carpeting and brick fireplace. In our previous house in San Antonio, I lived with my four siblings and parents in a three-bedroom home probably no more than fourteen hundred square feet — a single story tract home with linoleum floors. My three sisters shared a room together, and I shared one with my older brother. The home was a small neat red brick home with a one-car garage and a small, covered front porch.

Now we were moving into a brick, carpeted, two-story four-bedroom home with a fireplace and a detached two-car garage with two and a half baths and a large back yard! At ten years old, I didn't know how this really worked but I remembered figuring my parents had suddenly gotten rich.

There was no doubt my stepfather inherited a very strong work ethic. He married my mother, who already had three children (me being the youngest) from another marriage. Two more sisters were added along the way.

We lived more than twenty miles from downtown Houston, where my stepfather worked for a large national insurance company in middle management. Typically, he was gone in the mornings before I woke up and was home by 6:00 p.m. most nights. He wore a suit and tie to work every day, but never talked about his job during dinner which, like most families, was the only time the entire family was together.

One of the first chores I ever had was shining my stepfather's wing-tip lace dress shoes. He always had two pair — in black and brown. It was my job to make them shine and I pulled out the shoeshine kit every Sunday and took great pride in shining those two pairs of shoes for him for the week. After I was done with shining shoes, I was brought the golf clubs to clean from his weekly Saturday golf outings he took with his colleagues every weekend.

For all the differences I eventually had with my stepfather, there's no doubt he instilled a work ethic in me from an early age for which I will always be grateful. I don't think a work ethic is necessarily genetic. I think it is instilled or acquired.

My mother, who for most of my childhood was a stay-at-home mom, was always sure every detail for my stepfather was attended to, from having his suits cleaned, shirts pressed, coffee ready for the daily commute, and dinner on the table at the appointed time.

Most of the conversations I got to overhear from my parents regarding my stepfather's job were about who got what promotions, where someone was getting transferred to and why someone got passed over.

Since both my parents were smokers, they would sit out on the back patio on some nights and weekends and discuss the politics of the office at the giant insurance company. My parents were very involved socially in his company, attending any dinner or event that might help him advance in any way.

Looking back now, it seems apparent to me that my stepfather was in a corporate culture that was highly political and stressful. I can remember how ominous it sounded when they talked about a fellow worker who had been "passed over" for a promotion or transfer, which seemed to be the end of his or her advancement potential at the company.

I could always tell where the subject was going in their conversations when they lowered their voices to a whisper. My parents avoided those who didn't get that promotion or, in some cases, were demoted. It seemed it was hazardous to my stepfather's career to associate with those, even socially, who didn't appear to be on the same career trajectory as my stepfather. If you got "passed over," it was as if you had contracted *corporate leprosy*.

My stepfather had been transferred from St. Louis, where he started his career, to San Antonio, then to Houston, then to Sacramento (twice), then to Tampa, then to Hartford, then back to Houston. Fortunately, I was out of high school before he was transferred from Houston. I can remember my mother complaining about how they lost money every time they got transferred, despite the fact that the insurance company purchased their home when it didn't sell right away and paid for their relocation expenses. They were never really able to build equity in any of their homes because they were never in them long enough and, in most cases, they actually lost money to take the transfer and promotion.

I can recall two conversations when my parents were moving to California and then again to the home office in Connecticut. They complained about the cost of living compared to Texas, the substantial increase in taxes, and the cost of homes, yet they accepted the transfer. Most of these promotions were, in fact, a step backward financially when all elements were considered. In that environment, however, you did not turn down a transfer. To do so ended any chance of upward mobility. Despite the fact his job moved him away from her children, my mom never seemed to object and was loyal to my stepfather's career decisions.

While I was in high school, I worked at the insurance company one summer in the mailroom and got to see first-hand the respect others in the company had for him.

My stepfather was a true company man in every sense of the word. He would not even consider bringing home a paper clip from the office unless he was authorized or paid for it. When he talked about his company, he did so with pride. My stepfather was generally respected by all and eventually became a general manager and later a vice president.

Later in his career, a competitor purchased his employer. After thirty-five plus years as a company man, he had no idea what the future held for him during the merger. I remember well the angst he went through during the uncertainty that suddenly grasped his career.

After the merger, he sat in an office for months with no responsibilities. The vice president position he had held was given to a minority with a Harvard MBA at half his salary. Once one of the rising stars of the entire organization, he retired into oblivion. It was sad. It was disgusting. It wasn't fair. A man who had been a high performer, dedicated and loyal to his employer, didn't receive the same loyalty in return.

Sadly, my stepfather did not live long in retirement, as he never seemed to have a purpose or even a hobby. For a time, he had sixteen acres with a small pond about fifty miles out of town where he would spend a few days a week, but he eventually lost interest in that, too. Most days were spent watching the Golf Channel on television in his easy chair.

A highly respected man who was devoted to the company, who was at the office by 7:00 a.m. for thirty-five years, who dedicated his entire adult life to a single company, walked out for the last time with no thank you from his superiors and only the good wishes of the few surviving original fellow employees. Yes, there was a small party for him, but regular contact from fellow employees dwindled to just a few and only from his closest friends at the company.

Numerous indelible impressions were made on me as I watched my stepfather spend his entire career with a single company. The single largest impact was watching as he was dealt the harsh reality that, in the end, as an employee you do not control your own destiny, no matter your loyalty, political connections or past performance.

Today, it is unusual for employees to have this type of long-term tenure with a single employer. Most people have multiple employers over their lifetimes. The type of two-way loyalty many of us expect of our employers can quickly evaporate, even from well-intentioned employers, due to reasons beyond their control.

I learned, first and foremost, that I could never live in places I didn't want to live just because of a job. My parents did not choose to leave their kids and grandchildren and move to California with the high taxes and exorbitant housing costs. They did not choose to live in Hartford with its cold winters and corporate caste system that dominated their social life at the home office. These are both nice places for those who choose to live there, but my parents never would have chosen them if not for the job. They chose to take those transfers to further my stepfather's career or to avoid the sure corporate stigma attached to turning down a transfer or promotion.

I can remember my stepfather being presented on at least two occasions with opportunities to become a full partner in two very large insurance brokerages. He turned down both opportunities. The perceived security of a corporate job and regular paycheck outweighed his perceived risk of independence. Those two insurance brokers remain in business today many years later and appear to be thriving.

Instead, my stepfather reluctantly brought the moving company in once again, took a loss on the equity in the house and moved to Hartford. I never got the chance to ask him if he regretted this decision but, as proud as he was, he may never have admitted to me, or even to himself, that he should have jumped on one of those two opportunities. The lessons this taught me were invaluable and, unfortunately, at my stepfather's expense.

When reflecting on how short life on this earth really is, how sad would it be to live somewhere you didn't enjoy, far away from your family, just to keep a job? Yet it was common. To him, it was honorable to remain loyal to his employer and his role as a provider.

I remember asking my stepfather on a rainy Saturday afternoon as I helped him do a tune-up on our '71 Ford Maverick, if he didn't work for the insurance company, what would he do? His answer? He'd be a master plumber.

What?

I was stunned.

A plumber? Really? This Brooks Brothers three-piece suit corporate executive? I honestly don't know if my mother even knew this. His dream was to be a plumber in business for himself. He seemed to be pretty good with his hands and I think he would have enjoyed it.

He also did most of the mechanic work needed on our car and later, when we had two cars, he took care of both. He also did a lot of work around the house when things broke. I always thought it was to save money by not paying someone else, as money was always tight. In retrospect, I think he enjoyed it, although he would complain he didn't have the proper tools to do the jobs right, especially when it came to fixing the car. That frustration would bring out a fairly vicious temper, sometimes directed at me.

All these experiences became rooted in me and affect me to this day, as the experiences you have lived will do the same to you. I couldn't imagine spending my life working at a job I didn't like. I could never be forced to live somewhere I didn't want to live, military service notwithstanding.

Can you imagine spending your entire career devoted to an organization only to have it turn its back on you? How about living away from your kids or grandchildren?

It is possible that my stepfather, burdened with the responsibility of a family with five children, would never take the perceived risk to jump off and start his own business or take that partnership in one of the two brokerage firms. Maybe the time was never right. Maybe he was just "risk averse"; after all, he was in the risk management business (insurance).

Toward the end of his career, I pressed him about his corporate job versus being a business owner and he mentioned how many people worked for him, the size of his department budget he was responsible for, and the respect of colleagues.

He said, "It's like running my own business, without the risk."

With all due respect, I didn't argue but, since I already ran my own businesses by that time, I realized my stepfather was never really ready to take a risk. He had five kids and a wife to feed, plus a mortgage and bills. But even later, after me and my siblings grew up, he still clung to his corporate job.

The truth of the matter is, the higher you climb on the corporate ladder, the less stable your job is. In the end, the company didn't appreciate any of his contributions or his loyalty.

Statistics now prove out that few people will do what my stepfather did, working for the same employer thirty-plus years. Many move from job to job every five to six years.

Maybe he had no regrets. I never asked him.

Are you the type of person who puts your fate in others' hands?

Others will argue that you do it every day when you climb into your car or step onto a commercial jet.

There are many good corporations. I don't deny that. Many do great deeds in the community and are good corporate citizens. This book is not written to tear down those who choose this path. But, if you are like me, corporate America is not an option. What will you do with your life? It's never too late.

Lessons Learned:

▶ *Have the courage to pursue YOUR dreams.*

▶ *Your ultimate happiness is tied to pursuing your own path.*

▶ *When applying logic to the "work to retire" myth, it makes little practical sense.*

▶ *Don't expect your loyalty to an employer or big company to be reciprocal.*

▶ *The higher you climb in corporate America, the less stable your job becomes.*

CHAPTER 7

THE COLLEGE MAN

"I enjoyed high school and college, and I think I learned a lot, but that was not really my focus. My focus was on trying to figure out what businesses to start."

—*Steve Case*
Entrepreneur, Founder of AOL

I remember well during my high school years the emphasis put on me to attend college, but I can never remember anyone explaining the virtues of a college education, other than to get a good job.

So let's get this out of the way right up front. Our public educational system from grade school through major state-funded and private universities is designed (with very rare exceptions) to teach you to work for someone else, period.

I'm sensitive to the fact that I get castigated for my criticism of our public education system and the value of a college education. That being said, I encouraged my children to attend college, but for the right reasons. Two of my four children have college degrees. The other two had little interest in college, which to some degree (no pun intended), I can fully understand and relate to.

First of all, to me the most significant achievement of a college education is the fact that someone can set a goal and work to achieve it over a four-year (or thereabouts) period. For most of us, college required sacrifices. I can remember putting a quarter's worth of gas in my Torino to get to class. I always worked at something in college because I absolutely hated to be broke. Now, I never made much money and never had much more than pocket change, but having just a little bit of money gave me options.

Most of my friends and college roommates did not have to work, as their parents gave them money. I thank God mine didn't. Yes, they took care of the basics — tuition, room and board, etc. But my clothes, entertainment, books, etc. were all on me.

I can remember my first few weeks in college at Texas A&M University. Sitting in my college algebra class, panic hit. Although I graduated in the top 10 percent of my class in high school, I never really had to study. I would only study for tests — and that was only if I needed to. I thought I was smart!

During the first thirty minutes of the algebra class, the instructor put up equations that looked like some type of alien architecture to me. I knew right away I was in trouble, and my plans for the fun things I liked to do, especially sports and chasing girls, were in serious jeopardy.

The truth is, I was completely and utterly bored to death. I specifically went to college to learn how to make money. How in the heck was studying English Lit, Algebra and the other primary subjects that were also covered in high school going to benefit me, especially since I knew I didn't want to be an English teacher or an engineer?

It's funny; I was showing an employee how to figure out how to determine a mark-up on one of our telecom consulting services with an algebraic equation and it's one I probably learned as a sophomore in high school. Somehow I've built multi-million dollar businesses without advanced algebra.

Had I decided to become an engineer or an architect, I would have needed more advanced training in mathematics, but I knew that wasn't where I was going.

The most important math to me was always *counting money,* especially my own!

There was a time when I thought seriously about pre-law, so the basic classes during the first two years in college were a necessary evil to get an undergraduate degree to eventually go to law school. Then several of my friends who opted out of going to college came to see us and they had fancy new cars and money in their pockets. They had gone on to a trade or job. They weren't putting a quarter's worth of regular in their gas tanks. Some of them were preparing to take over a family business.

There were a lot of factors that contributed to me dropping out of college and not finishing. Do I wish I had finished? Sure I do. But within a year of finally giving up on the college experience and dropping out, I was in business with my older brother in our first airfreight business.

Texas A&M is a fantastic school, but it wasn't my first choice. But my stepfather had the ultimate say. After dropping out and earning the disfavor of my stepfather, I attempted to put myself through school. For someone who detested being constantly broke, you can guess how this went. My foray at the school that originally was my first choice, the University of Texas, was more short-lived than the first.

A defining moment came for me while I was attending an economics class I was not registered for. Yes, I found myself doing this more often than not. Heck, for me, sitting in an economics class was a thrill compared to the torture I endured in English literature and Algebra.

The economics class had about two hundred students in an amphitheater-styled auditorium. They didn't take attendance. It was perfect.

After about four of these classes, mostly taught by grad assistants, the professor made a rare appearance and delivered what I thought was an intriguing lecture but, of course, my inquiring mind had questions.

Unable to get my questions answered, I tried to make my way down to the podium after class, which was like a salmon swimming upstream against a horde of salmon swimming downstream. The professor was out the door behind the podium before I could get half way down the aisle.

I reversed course to swim with the rest of the salmon and, when I got outside, I ran around the building trying to find the professor. I finally caught a glimpse of him in the parking lot and made a beeline to him.

I finally caught up to Dr. Uptight Professor at his rusted-out, hippy-looking VW bus as he was opening the driver's side door. I could see the asphalt pavement through the floorboard, which was rusted completely through in some spots.

I don't remember exactly what he said to me except that he told me to contact one of his graduate assistants for any questions I had on his lecture. He was totally rude and arrogant!

As he backed out and drove away in a cloud of gray smoke, it looked like his VW bus was burning oil at a quart per minute. I was literally stunned, angry and depressed, all at the same time.

How in the world could an economics professor be so broke that I had nineteen- and twenty-year-old friends who had nicer cars than him? Surely an economics professor would be successful, wouldn't he? My goodness, he was teaching *Economics,* for God's sake! How could they let someone who was not successful teach Economics at a prestigious university?

I immediately went to the library to research the good professor. My research showed he had never owned a business and, in fact, had always been employed by the state or federal government. The university had someone teaching impressionable young minds about economics in a capitalistic society who, in fact, had *never* actually participated in the purest form of capitalism!

That was it for me. I was done.

The truth of the matter is that most college professors teach *theory*. Granted, there are some intellectual giants at universities all over the world. The trouble is, the vast majority have never applied their theories to the real world. This is especially true in business schools.

Does that mean that major university business schools have nothing to teach? Not at all. In fact, some schools, like the University of Houston, have recognized the need for a degree program in Entrepreneurship and, as of this writing, have the number one school in this field in the United States. Another is Lamar University. There is a growing interest from millennials in this type of degree path.

In speaking with other major universities that have expressed interest in a course or degree plan in this area, I am amazed at the resistance from university leadership. A degree program in Entrepreneurship is a real threat to the stuffed-shirt intellectuals.

But even schools with these degree paths couldn't have people like Steve Jobs, Michael Dell, or even me, teach a class. Why? We aren't *certified* teachers! We could be guest speakers, but not *accredited...* Of course, they would gladly take our money for an endowment. But they claimed they would lose their coveted accreditation for having someone like Jobs or Dell teach a class!

Academia is a microcosm of socialism. For all the so-called benefits of promoting tenure (where professors can't be fired) and unions, the typical university has become infested with so much political correctness that most have lost sight of their original purpose.

As much as I hate to say it, if you send a kid to a typical American university today, you will likely get back a little communist. My advice to someone going off to college: *question everything you are taught and who's teaching it!*

There is absolutely no balance in academia. Unless your child is well grounded in the values you endear, you might not recognize that child at graduation, as he or she will have leftist propaganda drilled into their impressionable young minds for four or more years.

Can you learn skills in college that translate into success in your own business? Sure. Problem solving, goal setting and human relation skills can and should be learned skills as a result of a college education.

Business school can also teach accounting basics, marketing and other valuable topics that could be helpful in starting and operating a business. The trick here is getting taught *applied* accounting, marketing and other relevant business subjects, meaning how are these subjects relevant for the students in their *own* businesses?

Another important aspect to a college education is that some people need that experience and time to mature. Not many are ready to start a self-sustaining business at eighteen years old.

Even though I knew I wanted a business at eighteen years old, I didn't have a clue how to get there. If nothing else, my brief college experience helped crystalize the desire to chase my dream.

Going to college for the sake of going to college isn't reason enough in my opinion for the financial investment. Many kids jump into a degree program without even knowing the hiring or income statistics for their chosen field. Liberal arts degrees, for example, pay very little in the job market compared to other degree programs. Couple the wrong degree choice with the huge debt of a six-figure student loan and it's hard to imagine what the individual was thinking. Financial literacy is covered in the next chapter.

I would never discourage people from going to college provided they can pay for it. Some of the best students are those who take on a full-time job and go to college part-time. Having the experience of different jobs while working toward a degree often helps students figure out what they really want to do. Also, there is nothing wrong with getting the first two years of basic classes out of the way at a community college; just make sure the classes will transfer to the university you plan to attend.

If you have to get a student loan to go to college, you are probably an ideal candidate for the full-time job and part-time college student scenario instead of racking up a huge debt. I have seen many students change majors because of changes in their interest levels, and now they have debt for classes they will not get credit for.

If you plan to be a lawyer, doctor, architect, engineer or other professional, you have no choice. You have to get a degree and, if you then want to focus on building your own business in your chosen field, you have the background, certifications and degrees necessary.

It's also never too late to go back to school, provided you can meet your financial requirements and pay your bills. If your chosen business requires a degree, go back part time if you have to.

Do you have to have a degree to be successful in business? Absolutely not. Does it help? Sure, but it doesn't guarantee your success, either. From the standpoint of always having the ability to get a job, a degree looks good on your resume.

A degree can also open doors for you for entry-level jobs that require a degree and can be the springboard you need to launch your own business in that field. After I dropped out, I got a job in the airfreight business. A year later, at my urging and planning, my older brother and I started our first airfreight business. The same thing can happen for you. Learn your new business from ground level and start your own.

Also helpful is that some universities have very powerful alumni who tend to look for their fellow alumni to fill open positions. They also tend to do business with their own. Universities with connected and powerful alumni such as Texas, Texas A&M,

Stanford, Yale, Harvard, Rice, Notre Dame, Illinois, Northwestern and many others fit this category.

Does an MBA help? I believe it does, but is it necessary to have an advanced degree to become successful in your own enterprise? No.

Lessons Learned:

▶ *A college degree is NOT necessary to become successful in business.*

▶ *College can help you, providing well-rounded basic knowledge as well as problem-solving skills and goal-setting habits.*

▶ *The entire public education system is set up by academia to focus individuals on obtaining employment, not participating in the free enterprise system.*

▶ *Some schools, like the University of Houston, Lamar University and others, offer degree programs in Entrepreneurship.*

▶ *Do not go into debt to go to college. If you have to get a student loan, you likely should work full time and go to school part time. This is especially true if you are relatively undecided on your path in life or, stated in simpler terms, what degree you are pursuing.*

▶ *If the thought of years in school again sends shivers up your spine, consider taking specific classes that may help in your endeavor. Classes like accounting, marketing and others are typically taught at your local community college.*

CHAPTER 8

ARE YOU FINANCIALLY ILLITERATE?

"I have done stupid with a lot of zeros on the end of it. I know what it looks like."

—*Dave Ramsey*
Entrepreneur, Author, TV and Radio Host
Creator of Financial Peace University

This book is not a book about personal finance per se. There are many very good books that teach the responsible handling of money. That being said, I cannot stress enough the importance of practicing sound financial principles to first put yourself in position to take advantage of your ambitions, and then maintaining those principles so your business takes care of you and your family.

Of all the serious problems with our public education system (and there are many), I see one continual issue that manifests itself at an early age.

Most Americans are, for the most part, financially *illiterate*. Our educational system doesn't teach financial basics like balancing a checkbook, savings, the dangers of credit card debt, etc.

Most Americans live above their means, financing their *lifestyle* with debt. The vast majority don't have an *income* problem; they have a *spending* problem (*sounds like our federal government!*). If this thinking isn't fixed when the income is modest, it will manifest itself greatly when or if the income grows. If the income drops, even a little, it becomes an immediate crisis.

Here's a tidbit: If you make a million dollars this year and you spend one million and one dollars this year, you are *broke*!

I have seen, time and time again, where the financially undisciplined get themselves in more debt when their income grows. I had this disease when I was a young business owner, because the opportunity to finance more debt becomes easier to do as your income grows.

The financially undisciplined entrepreneur will not be self-employed for long, or will bounce from crisis to crisis and from failure to failure but likely never realize what the root cause of the failures are.

The most expensive financial lessons I have learned in business have all been caused by my lack of financial literacy at the time. There are certain financial laws that can't be broken — or you suffer the consequences. The two main culprits are debt and spending more than you take in.

For those who have a burning desire to own a business and gain financial independence, lack of financial discipline will sink your dream faster than a torpedo sinks a ship. There are undoubtedly millions of great business ideas that never got off the ground or failed as quickly as they were launched because their businesses mirrored their owners' bad personal financial habits.

Many will never consider starting a business because of the debt they have. Afraid to lose that "secure" paycheck, they are forced to put their dreams on hold simply because they don't understand financial basics.

There are telltale clues that should be warning signs to your financial future regardless of whether you have a job or start a business. Those warning signs include one or more of the following factors:

1. No savings or emergency cash (4-6 months' worth)
2. One small crisis away from disaster (car repair, house repair, etc.)
3. Paying minimums only on credit cards
4. Carrying large credit card debt
5. Unpaid student loans
6. Inability to pay bills when due
7. No tithing or giving to charity
8. Financing lifestyle or luxury items (Status: Keeping up with the Joneses)
9. House poor/car poor
10. Lack of health insurance
11. Lack of life insurance
12. Believe they deserve vacations they cannot afford (entitlement)
13. Bad credit
14. Mortgage with a variable interest rate (usually done to qualify for a home they wouldn't otherwise have qualified for)

Debt is the most serious impediment to starting a business. When you have debt, you likely do not have the cash to start a business or can't afford to take a step backward in lifestyle for a period in order to gain your freedom, as is sometimes necessary when launching a new venture. If you are heavily in debt with a mortgage or rent, car payments, credit card debt and student loans, you likely are using all available cash from your paychecks to service that debt.

For some, this is exactly the reason they go into business. Frustrated with their inability to make their income rise or pay their bills, they start a second business to supplement income. However, if the laws of financial management don't get fixed permanently, the amount of extra income that is achieved will never be enough to fix the problem.

This does not at all mean businesses can't be started on a shoe-string or by bootstrapping. It depends on the business you're trying to launch. The more capital-intensive the business is, the more important it is that your finances be in good condition.

For some, it makes more sense to test the waters with a part-time business to see if their business model will work before they give up that regular paycheck and dive in full time. There are millions of successful businesses that started as a hobby or to develop a second income that grew into the owners' primary source of income.

However, for any business I started, it was *never* the right time for our finances. We started having children just about the time we launched our airfreight business. Like us, you may *never* have the ideal circumstances. But we didn't let the facts get in our way.

The most important thing to remember regarding the timing is that it's up to you to make it happen. What are you trying to achieve? If your *why* is big enough, you will figure out the details.

In today's environment, most young Americans believe they deserve the same lifestyles that may have taken their parents twenty to thirty years to achieve. Society today is an instant society, with most expecting immediate satisfaction in almost every endeavor they seek. Unfortunately, business doesn't always reward you instantaneously, except in the satisfaction of knowing you are your own boss!

There are many books that deal with getting out of debt that provide quality instruction. When people tell me they can't pay their bills, the first thing I ask them is what do they have that they can sell? Sell anything you don't need and start paying down the smallest debts to the largest. With the monthly payments freed up by paying off the small debts, pay more toward the largest debt or the one with the highest interest rate. Some renowned financial experts refer to this as a *debt-reduction snowball effect.*

Many newlywed couples finance a car at a young age. If the money for the monthly payments on the vehicle was instead invested in a modest mutual fund or other safe investment, that same car payment, alternatively invested, would likely result in a million dollar or more savings account by age sixty.

Don't believe me? Look it up. Compounding interest and reinvestment of dividends and earnings has an exponential effect. Ask someone today if they would like to have $50,000 right now, or a penny a day doubled for 30 days. After 30 days, with a penny doubled daily, you would have $10.7 million. That is the power of the compounding effect.

When you go into debt to finance a depreciating asset like a new car, you have robbed yourself of the power of compounding interest. But that new car smell is just so inviting!

To be financially astute, it's important to know the difference between assets and liabilities. A home is generally an asset; however, if you have to finance it and ultimately pay for it over thirty years, how wise is the investment? Sure, as of the writing of this book, there is the tax deduction for mortgage interest, but politicians continue to play with the limits of that deduction. Our government and politicians are essentially financially illiterate. The debt is unsustainable and sooner or later there will be a reckoning. What better reason to get a business started and start protecting you and your family?

Generally speaking, I advise folks that, if they can't pay the amortized mortgage over a 15-year loan, then they likely can't afford the home they are trying to buy. Harsh? Maybe. But interest rates are always more favorable to shorter-term mortgages.

Never, never, never agree to a mortgage that has a variable interest rate. Did I say never? Yes. Never. Ever. Even as attractive as that initial interest rate might be, don't be fooled by the lower payment, which is temporary. As the government becomes more financially unstable, the more at risk you are of being priced right out of your home, unable to make payments when the interest rates rise which, despite the manipulation of the Federal Reserve, will surely happen while you are in your next 30-year mortgage.

Credit cards? Simply don't use them. Few people are disciplined enough to pay their balances at the end of the month. Nowadays, even rental car companies will accept check cards with Visa™ or MasterCard™ logos. Only a very small percentage of credit card holders have the discipline to use their cards wisely enough that they can pay off the balance at the end of each month.

When I tried to get my arms around this concept in my mid-twenties, I used to deduct any amount I put on a credit card from my check register as if the cash was already gone (this was before debit cards existed). That way I would have enough at month's end to pay for all my credit card purchases.

This habit also kept me from spending more than I should, as I never wanted to see a negative balance in my register or not have enough to pay the electric bill, etc.

Studies have proven that we spend less if we have cash than with plastic. I always have some cash with me. It's been a lifelong habit so I would avoid using credit cards for silly purchases. Mentally, it is harder to part with cash than using a credit or debit card.

Always balance your bank statements within 48 hours of receiving them. Nowadays, with bill payment options, online banking and opt-in emails, you should always know how much cash you have in your accounts. To this day, I look at all my cash balances daily, as most come to me in emails from banks wherein I opted to get a daily email update showing balances and what has cleared the night before. Banks do make mistakes, sometimes fairly large ones. Some have limits for when you can correct their mistakes, so it is important to balance your accounts monthly.

Status is kryptonite to entrepreneurship. It keeps you from reaching your dreams and gives you a false and hollow sense of accomplishment.

Having a car or home you can't afford makes it much harder to go into business for yourself and, to this day, I believe it contributed to my stepfather never becoming an independent business owner.

Status can also cause you to be *house poor*. Buying a house you can't afford is either bad financial management or trying to impress others and, in most cases, both.

My definition of *status* is buying things you don't need or can't really afford to impress people you don't know.

If what you drive, the home you live in, the jewelry and clothes you wear and the country club you attend are keeping you from living on 80 percent of what you bring home, you will **never** make it as an entrepreneur. There will come a time sooner than you think where you need that extra computer, delivery van, piece of equipment, employee or machinery. Your available capital will be tied up in lifestyle purchases you likely financed to quench your need for that mythical self-worth deception called *status*.

Fake it 'til you make it?

I don't recommend it.

In fact, depending on what business you go into, many times customers and even your own employees can be put off by extravagant items. Customers may begin to think you charge too much and employees may feel you are shortchanging them by spending money on personal luxury items instead of needed items for the business.

How many times do you see this? People buy cars, clothes, jewelry or homes they can't afford? People who are house poor or car poor who live from one crisis to the next? Murphy's law dictates that something inevitably happens: a car breaks down or a washing machine goes on the blink. Instead of having a rainy day fund, a few hundred-dollar repair causes a major financial crisis.

I had a friend who had a very nice Mercedes. He had a fender bender in a parking lot but never could afford the deductible to get his fender and quarter panel fixed. He drove his $75,000 Mercedes for over two years with his right front fender crunched!

Not far from my current home is a large home with absolutely zero landscaping. And it's been that way for years. My guess is the homeowners are so burdened with their mortgage payments they cannot afford to plant a shrub or two.

To get to the point where you are *unemployable*, you may have to live without status symbols until you can afford them. Throughout our country's history, many entrepreneurs, merchants and business owners have actually lived in the businesses they started. You used to be able to find these businesses, like the hardware store, bakery, tailor and others, on Main Street. They weren't worried about status. They were worried about making a profit, putting food on the table, serving the community and surviving.

How bad do you want to be self-employed? Are you willing to re-invest in your business and do without the latest gadget, trendy designer clothes, or new car? How much is your freedom worth? Are you willing to delay your gratification?

If you can't afford it (meaning buying it without financing it), don't buy it. You can't eat a home, or a car for that matter. Sometimes, to get a venture launched successfully, you have to give up that artificial status, which makes the real thing that much more enjoyable when you achieve it! *The only people you should be interested in impressing are the people who buy your products or services.*

Rarely mentioned in many business books is the importance of maintaining your credit. At a point early in one of my ventures,

I went to several banks to get a loan on our substantial accounts receivable. The business had the financial statements to support a line of credit, but my personal credit history was not ideal. Since most banks depend on the small business owner to guarantee the loan or credit line, my personal credit score sank any opportunity I had to get a badly needed loan. I was forced to factor my accounts receivable at a substantial increase in costs versus a bank loan.

Many people I have met in life have had plans to go into business but could never seem to make the big step off the false security of a paycheck from a job. Living above their means kept them living paycheck to paycheck and thus shackled to a job.

I remember the story of Sam Walton, founder of Wal-Mart, driving a used pick-up truck to work every day while he was one of the richest men in America.

I learned the hard way that I needed to delay lifestyle purchases and not go into unnecessary debt for items that really weren't assets or didn't advance my business.

When I finally understood some basic financial concepts, I drove our delivery van to and from work. It wasn't pretty, but I was damned proud of the company name on that van. I traded in a BMW that I really couldn't afford and didn't need. That van with *my* company name was the only status symbol I needed. I made a promise to myself that my freedom, and a full pantry and refrigerator, were more important to me and my family than any house or car.

Nobody likes to practice *delayed gratification*, meaning to put off until later things you might like to have *now*, to be able to afford to invest in growing your business to reap the rewards later.

I can remember we badly needed a new couch, but my airfreight business also needed a few more computers. This was a no-brainer for me. The computers made me money, the couch made me fat! My wife Rose was a trooper, never complaining about the sacrifices we made. She remembers a very brief period before we were married when I was an employee of an airfreight company and how miserable I was — and how miserable I made everyone around me. That was the last time in my life I ever worked for someone else as an employee, leaving the world of the employed at twenty-one years old forever!

One of the hardest struggles I had was understanding that, no matter how much income was coming in, I had to pay *me* first with whatever came in. If you can't live on 80 percent of your income (no matter the source), you are living above your means. Let that sink in for a moment…

If you can't live on 80 percent of your income, you are financing a lifestyle you can't afford. Period.

Ten percent of your earnings need to go into savings, without fail. This is your rainy day fund. It's not to be used for vacations or lifestyle. The other ten percent should go to wherever your conscience decides, whether it be church or charities. Save four to six months' equivalent to your income for an emergency fund that you can access easily before your consider contributing to a retirement fund. This is the fund you use to pay for that transmission that goes out, an unexpected appliance breakdown, or an emergency room visit, etc. That may seem like an impossible task for some who live paycheck to paycheck. Take small steps. Get a plan and get started.

I was twenty-eight before I started understanding these basic financial principles. They weren't taught to me in any school and I didn't inherit them. I got them by reading books and associating with people more successful than me.

I had two business failures before age twenty-eight, one of them fairly significant. I attribute these failures to a lack of financial literacy. My business created substantial gross revenues, but I applied the same failed financial logic that I used in my personal life to my businesses — with the same results.

I've had cars repossessed. I have had the IRS show up at our place of business and our home. These circumstances were ALL avoidable with some practically applied financial literacy.

Are you willing to drive your current vehicle for two more years? Do you need to sell it to get out from under the car payments and buy a used car? Do you really need the latest gadget? Can you find that business suit at a discount store? What does your business need instead? Take care of your business so it can take care of you and your family.

When people live above their means, they limit their options. I always remind people that a paycheck is never guaranteed. Where would they be if the paychecks suddenly stopped? How long could they maintain their current lifestyle before they couldn't pay their mortgage or rent, their car note, credit card bills? A month? A week?

As my income rose, I found it became easier to finance things. At one point in my early twenties, we had five cars. Yes, you read that correctly. Five. And three homes. They were all financed with minimum down payments. My airfreight company was grossing over $1 million. Both my brother and I were taking fat paychecks from the business (this is different than paying yourself by putting money in savings) and spending every dime, thinking the business was bulletproof. I was making more money than most people I knew or hung out with, and I thought it would never end.

Then the mid-eighties oil bust hit Houston.

We took a forty percent hit in revenue, which had we been smarter was totally survivable, except for the fact that I hadn't planned on this type of hiccup, either in my business or my personal finances.

To make matters worse, I listened to bad advice about our payroll taxes. The IRS didn't care.

It was a humbling experience. It was embarrassing. I'm sure many were glad to see that cocky twenty-something-year-old lose his rear. The IRS debt hounded me for years. Since my brother never signed a single tax return, he miraculously escaped the IRS tyranny. To this day, the fear of failure associated with that experience is still a factor in my motivation.

Like most entrepreneurs, we tend to view something like this as a temporary setback. Did I quit and go get a job? No. Did my wife want me to? Probably. But she knew me all too well, and she believed in me. Did we argue? Sure. When money is tight, it impacts every area of our lives and we all know that financial strife is one of the top reasons people end up in divorce.

Knowing that it was my responsibility to put food on the table, my wife will tell anyone that asks that somehow, some way, I found a way. My kids may not have been eating steak, but they never went to bed hungry.

The IRS hauled away desks and computers right from under

my employees into a moving van on a Monday morning. I lost my airfreight company.

The next day, I was starting another one.

Lessons Learned:

▶ *Although financial stress is many times the reason people start their own businesses, practicing basic financial management principles lessens the failure rate.*

▶ *Most people live above their means (including the federal government and many state/local governments).*

▶ *Never, never, never finance "lifestyle" purchases. (examples: jewelry and vacations, etc.).*

▶ *"Status" is the antithesis of sound financial principles and is a leading contributor to business failures as well as personal financial failures.*

▶ *Learn to live on 80 percent of your take-home pay.*

▶ *Put off major expenses that aren't critical to the advancement of your business.*

▶ *Always, always, always know your EXACT cash position, account balances and debt.*

▶ *Always know your credit score. The object of having a good credit score is to have it as an asset if and when the time comes that you need it for growth/expansion capital, cash flow or payroll. A good credit score is NOT to be used to finance "lifestyle" purchases.*

▶ *No matter how good your business model is or how much profit it generates, it will never survive long-term without you practicing sound financial practices.*

▶ *Use qualified professionals for accounting and taxes! But don't be afraid to get second opinions.*

CHAPTER 9

THE GROWTH OF THE MICRO BUSINESS

"What do you need to start a business? Three simple things: know your product better than anyone, know your customer, and have a burning desire to succeed."

—*Dave Thomas*
Founder of Wendy's®

A micro business is a business that is either part-time or has no more than two employees. According to the U.S. Census website, micro businesses make up 95 percent of the twenty-eight million businesses tracked by the federal government.

Many of these business start off as a result of a hobby or special interest by the owner.

How many times have you seen someone who is good at baking start a cupcake or wedding cake business? Surely you've seen the dog lover who starts a grooming or pet-sitting business? Another example is someone who is good with computers or works in IT who always gets asked to help someone with a computer virus or email and enjoys it so much they do it after hours or on weekends.

These small businesses are the backbone of the mighty American economic engine.

Businesses that revolve around the things you love to do are typically the easiest to start. Many times, if it is a hobby, you probably have many of the items needed to start.

Some deep introspection is required for anyone wanting to start a business. Many potential business owners look at the businesses that can make them the most money and start there. For them, the dream is the outcome of owning that business, but not necessarily the *love* of working that business.

I didn't go into the telecom business because I dreamed of doing so since I was a child. I saw it as an opportunity at the time to capitalize on an industry that was deregulating and thought it had the possibility of creating *residual* income. And, I actually like the business!

Over the years I have come to love the niche we carved out of the telecom industry. We literally pioneered an entire multi-billion dollar sub-category of telecommunications now known as *telecom expense management.*

I loved the outdoors, hunting, fishing, basketball, racquetball, dogs, golf, family and college football, but I wasn't clever enough to figure out how to make a good living from any of those hobbies and interests.

I recently opened a dancehall and recording venue because of my love of Texas music and Texas music artists.

For me, I needed to develop a business so I could enjoy those things. But, at the end of the day, you have to see yourself doing whatever you choose on a full-time basis. I could see myself in telecommunications, just like I could see myself running an air-freight business better than my previous employers. I have to say,

I liked both businesses. Both are highly competitive and require some very distinct business skills. I like taking accounts away from my competitors and the entire machinery involved with spinning the multiple plates of accounting, marketing, management and building customer and vendor relationships.

If your idea of a micro business is just to make an extra few hundred or thousand dollars a month, then go for it. However, if the intent is to develop a business that can replace your primary income, you must look at your potential micro business from that perspective. If you are blazing a new trail nobody has ventured onto yet, you may not really know if it can grow to a level to support you full time until you try.

First, does your idea for a micro business have the capacity at some point to replace your current income? This takes a very unemotional approach to assessing the marketability of your micro business idea. I have always found it easiest to assess an opportunity when I break it down into granular components. For example, if you were the baker mentioned earlier, how many wedding cakes and cupcakes would you have to bake monthly to replace that income? But, before you can really figure that out, it is imperative you know how much it costs you to make a single wedding cake or cupcake, to the penny, then how much you should charge so you can figure out your profit per unit.

One of the most common reasons businesses fail is because the owners never really know how much it costs to provide the product or service. Because they don't know, they price their product or service too cheaply and, in many cases, they sell their product or service for a loss and don't ever fully realize it until it's too late.

If I were the baker, I would figure out what my base wedding cake is. Is it a three-tier? How much would I spend in flour, sugar, eggs, etc. to make it? How long should it bake? How much are the utilities to keep an oven at 350 degrees for two hours? Yes, I'm serious about figuring out your *entire* overhead or cost of goods, and you should be, too!

I would price my competition and compare. What would make my cakes better so I could charge more than my competitors? Could I produce the cake sooner and therefore be able to charge more, by offering an *emergency cake service,* for instance? How many times has someone forgotten to order the birthday cake?

As a general rule, if you can't make a 40 percent gross profit on your product or service, you have it priced too cheaply. Even 40 percent is very narrow and does not allow much wiggle room to recover from inevitable unforeseen nasty surprises.

I see people frequently jump into a micro business with zero research on their competitors. Ask yourself if you can explain how your product or service is better in twenty seconds or less. And, if your answer is "mine is cheaper," you will have a harder time becoming successful. The ability to sell your product for less than competitors should be because you developed a better and less expensive way to make it (or buy it wholesale), not that you're willing to make less profit margin than the business down the street. What is your value add? What makes you unique?

Do your cakes taste better? Are they gluten-free? Are they made from organic flour and eggs? See where I'm going here? What you want to do is build enough value into your product or service so your customers will happily pay you *more* than your competitors.

If you're currently living paycheck to paycheck, but have a great idea for a micro business, where do you find the money to start, even if it's a small-time operation in the beginning?

Assuming you've done your research on competitors and the market viability of your idea, coming up with the money to start a micro business for most people comes from examples of one or a combination below:

1. Savings.

2. Credit cards (not recommended, but there are many examples of successful entrepreneurs who used this route initially). Only use this if you have proven financial literacy.

3. Family (be very careful here… this is covered in a later chapter).

4. Friends (same as family above…).

5. Business loan from a bank or credit union.

6. Personal loan from a bank or credit union.

7. Home equity loan (not generally recommended at this stage).

8. Crowdfunding (this is a new and exciting phenomenon in the Gig Economy).

9. Income tax refund.

10. Sell something… sell that boat you haven't used in two years, the antiques in your garage, your old sports equipment, etc. Have a garage sale! I have always been shocked at what we cleared in profit in our garage sales years ago.

As you can see, there are plenty of places to look for raising money for your new micro business.

Assuming you are starting your micro business as a home-based business, you will be able to capitalize on two of the last federal tax breaks available to American taxpayers.

First, it's important for you to understand that if you are getting a sizeable tax refund every year that only means you are paying too much in your tax contributions every pay period. Congratulations, you have just given the over-bloated federal government an interest-free loan for a year.

At any time, you can change your W-4 "allowances" that determine your taxes every pay period. You have the right to go to your employer and fill out a new W-4 to increase your allowances, thus reducing the taxes paid every pay period. This will instantly increase your take-home pay.

Use the link below to find a calculator to determine how more allowances claimed will impact your take-home pay: http://apps.irs.gov/app/withholdingcalculator/.

Many people make the mistake of attributing "allowances" to "dependents," which is not the same thing.

If you are able to operate your micro business from your home, you now qualify for home office deductions. Generally, you will be able to deduct all expenses associated with the space you use in your home to conduct that business. I highly recommend you dedicate a room if possible but, if not, a specific "area" of the home for your business. The proportionate space used for this business as compared to the total square feet of the home is what is used to deduct a portion of your mortgage interest, homeowners' insurance, repairs, maintenance, utilities, etc.

The second large tax break still available to you as a micro business owner is the Schedule C expense deduction. If you start your business as a sole proprietor (as opposed to a corporation, for example), you will be able to list the direct expenses of the business on your tax return. If your micro business has a loss, it will decrease your taxable income as the Schedule C losses come directly off your gross wages or income.

I'm not proposing these simply as tax strategies; however, millions of people using these strategies have decreased their tax liability by simply attempting to operate a business.

I highly recommend you seek professional tax advice from a competent and qualified CPA or tax professional that advises small businesses and startups before deploying any of these strategies.

One word of caution that I will detail in a later chapter: *The IRS looks at Schedule C expenses and home office deductions carefully.* You must make sure the business expenses are legitimate and docu-ment, document, document. Your tax professional should be able to help you with your bookkeeping system. There are also many online and off-the-shelf, easy-to-operate software programs for this purpose.

Gerald wasn't a very good golfer but he loved to play. He was intrigued by antique golf clubs and his wife always complained about how much space his collection took up in the garage. Collecting golf clubs had become his hobby, and he went to flea markets, garage sales, estate sales and anywhere he could to buy antique golf clubs.

As the price of golf clubs exploded in the early 2000s, Gerald noticed he had friends asking him to find a specific two- or three-year-old set of irons or woods. The major golf club manufacturers came out with new models every year and the older models were no longer in stores.

At first, when he found a particular set someone was looking for, he would just buy them and sell them to his friends or acquaintances for what he paid for them.

As with many micro business owners, Gerald was forced to find an alternate source of income. Gerald's first sign that his employer had some problems was when overtime was no longer approved. He had gotten used to the extra 15-plus hours of overtime he was getting every pay period. So used to it, in fact, he did like most people and structured his lifestyle to depend on it. Next came the announcement that health insurance cost increases were going to have to be made up by the employees, a full 20 percent increase to Gerald. The final straw came during a Christmas holiday; he was furloughed for a week between Christmas and New Year's, unpaid!

All these events happened within a six-month time frame. Gerald's wife already worked. For Gerald, panic set in. He could no longer cover all the family's monthly bills.

To Gerald's credit, he immediately began selling any items he didn't need. He had a garage sale, but decided to put many of his golf clubs and especially some of the complete sets on eBay and Craigslist. The first few complete sets sold quickly, to his surprise. The bidding for these sets was fast and furious.

Gerald was shocked. Some of these complete sets he bought for as little as $25 yet, when bidding was complete, sold for $300 or more! He sold ten complete sets in ten days, as well as some one-offs and unusual clubs. He didn't list his most prized antique clubs.

Gerald immediately recognized the opportunity. He placed his own ad on Craigslist: "I buy complete set golf clubs same day, in cash."

Gerald began to scour every second-hand store, garage and estate sale with any free time he had to build his inventory.

The result? Within six months, Gerald sold over 200 complete iron and wood sets, as well as over 500 individual irons, putters and wood golf clubs. Gerald made more in six months' part-time than he made at his full-time job the year before.

Gerald's business grew, and he now operates a website to buy/sell golf clubs. Despite the fact that most major retail golf stores now buy/sell used clubs as well as new, Gerald's micro business flourished. He has opened two small retail stores where customers can come in and browse the hundreds of used clubs, trade clubs, place an order for a club or set they are looking for, or sell the clubs they have for immediate cash.

Gerald has an incredible network of "pickers." He no longer goes to garage or estate sales, but has dozens who go for him with a list of what Gerald will pay them cash for and how much. If these pickers can buy the clubs cheaply enough, they have a ready-made instant sale to Gerald. They also bring him used balls that he resells.

Gerald takes special pride in the fact that he was able to outfit two local high school golf teams (both boys and girls) with complete, slightly used golf club sets.

He has expanded his business now to make custom clubs in his two retail locations as well as sell new golf accessories such as golf bags. His customer following is almost cult-like. He left his union electrician job within a year, and his wife and kids now help with the family business. His online business is still larger than his retail sales because his customer base is global, and he ships clubs to such far-away places as Dubai and Greenland.

Gerald's reasons for starting his micro business are very typical. Backed into a corner, he discovered a niche from his hobby that ultimately developed into a family business.

Lessons Learned:

▶ *Most micro businesses are started from hobbies or particular areas of knowledge or interest.*

▶ *Micro businesses have extreme flexibility and many are run from home.*

▶ *Many micro businesses are started out of necessity or to supplement incomes.*

▶ *Micro businesses have less than two employees, can be started and operated part-time, and typically do not have large investment criteria.*

▶ *The basics of operating a business don't change just because it's a micro business.*

▶ *There are big tax advantages with a home-based business and operating a micro business as a Schedule C business, but you must consult a tax professional.*

▶ *There has likely never been a better time in history to start a micro business due to technology advancements, connectivity, the Internet and social media.*

CHAPTER 10

YOU, INC. — THE SALES ENTREPRENEUR

"A mediocre idea that generates enthusiasm will go further than a great idea that inspires no one."

—Mary Kay Ash, 1918 -2001
Founder of Mary Kay Cosmetics®
Billionaire Entrepreneur

According to government statistics, salespeople on average make more money than most categories of employment. Those who can turn a sales career into entrepreneurship do even better.

My employees have heard this saying from me over the years and, to some, I'm sure it drives them crazy, *"Very few people know how to hunt something down, kill it, then drag it home."*

That is my definition of a true sales entrepreneur.

Many entrepreneurs find financial success and independence through the sheer capacity of their own performance.

I can definitely relate to the attraction of independence. After selling my last airfreight business and jumping into the telecommunications industry, I was an independent contract channel sales manager for a Chicago-based telecom company that was exploding with the advent of deregulation.

My business was similar to an independent agent who received generous overrides from recruiting professional telecom sales people to sell this firm's telecommunications products and services.

It was straight commission only. I didn't report to anyone and my hours were my own, as were my expenses. I succeeded or failed based on the results I achieved by the sales agents I recruited and trained. It was very lucrative, and the telecom industry in the late 1990s was a modern version of the Wild West.

I have always found great opportunities in business where there is the most chaos. We educated corporate telecom users, reduced their costs and got paid very well for doing so.

Yes, I was in business for myself. I was my only employee. Just like any other business, I had expenses, which ranged from travel expenses to advertising for the hiring of new sales agents.

Today, there are many independent sales people who would rather be their own sales entrepreneur than anything they can imagine.

Real estate agents are a perfect example. Working strictly on commission, they bear the expense of an office, advertising, and expenses. Many are successful enough to get a broker's license and hire other agents from whom they receive overrides on their sales. Additionally, many agents operate from home, never needing a traditional office.

Personally, I never would have considered a sales position that had a salary as the only compensation or worse — a position as a regular employee with a limit on my income. For other *Renegade Capitalists*® like me, it is very important that I have no ceiling to my earnings potential.

The financially literate sales entrepreneur will not be enslaved by base salary limitations. Those who are financially *illiterate* will be limited in their choice of sales positions, forced to take a job with limited potential but just enough base salary to cover their bills. The less overhead you have as debt, the more wide open your choices and thus the more capacity you have for a straight commission career with no limitation on your income ceiling.

When I interview potential sales people, they can disqualify themselves by asking more questions about a base salary than the income potential of our sales plan. Peak performers always want to know the income potential and true professionals only need a base salary if the sales cycle is extremely long.

A recurring theme you will see throughout this book is the attraction of residual income, whether a particular product generates repeat sales or income is generated through the production of others, such as in my early venture into telecommunications.

Independent insurance sales reps are another good example. My life insurance agent gets paid an annual or monthly residual for my life insurance policies for as long as I keep them. I love the idea that you can continue to get paid over and over for a single sale.

The old stereotypes of sales professionals will likely die with my generation. Today's professional sales entrepreneur is well trained, organized, highly motivated, connected and armed with information (consultative).

Some of the best sales people I have ever known were not born with the gift of gab. Sales are, and always have been, about the structured understanding of the law of averages, the ability to relate to people of all kinds and the talent to identify the customer's problem and the solution. Successful sales entrepreneurs are about preparedness meeting the right opportunities. Gone are the outdated methods of trying to "manipulate" a customer to buy something as a slick sales trick.

To find the right opportunities, a sales entrepreneur uses the law of averages to dial up the compensation he or she desires. It is the same methodology I explained with the wedding cake baker. You must know your cost of goods. As a sales entrepreneur in the telecom industry, I learned that I would eventually contract four out of ten sales people I recruited and, of those, only two would actually generate any sales. I knew the average production per month that came from my sales reps. Knowing this, I could easily calculate the numbers I needed to achieve for a particular income goal.

I don't believe professional sales entrepreneurs are born; they're made. None of us is born with the habits necessary to become gifted sales entrepreneurs. These are learned attributes. I have seen some of the most unlikely personalities achieve great success in sales because they master their habits, know their products inside and out, believe in those products and take immense pride and satisfaction in solving problems for their clients.

Emerging markets and industries going through some form of chaos are usually fertile areas for the sales entrepreneur to make a lot of money. Also, mature industries can be lucrative if you can find a new twist or solution. Don't ever forget that sometimes we buy from people simply because we *like them*!

I have been fortunate enough to be in two emerging markets right after deregulation (the airfreight and telecommunications industries). Although I can't say I sat around as a kid and dreamed of being in either of these industries, I thoroughly enjoyed finding unique solutions and differentiators that we created that made those businesses fun and lucrative for me.

Being as competitive as I am by nature, I really enjoyed taking an account from a competitor or being first to market with a unique solution to a problem for my customers.

The professional sales entrepreneur sees himself or herself as the liaison for the customer with the firms, products or services they are selling.

When considering a career as a sales entrepreneur, know who is going to pay you. If it is a company, is it reputable and stable?

Make 100 percent certain you have a contract. Unfortunately, most industries are littered with companies who changed the compensation plan unilaterally, and always to the detriment of the salesperson.

Check references, including customers, but especially other commissioned sales people.

Do you absolutely believe in the product or service? I truly believe you can't be successful representing something you don't believe in. Your potential customers will see right through you and you will have a hard time motivating yourself to practice the successful habits of a professional sales entrepreneur.

Take advantage of any training provided. If none is provided, invest in yourself and get the necessary training. Don't ever think your training is over. When you stop learning you can expect your sales to go backward.

Time management is the single most important skill for success for a sales entrepreneur. Time is truly money in this profession and everything else is secondary to being in front of qualified prospects on a daily basis.

Prospecting is the hunt. You should *enjoy* the hunt! Those who get proficient at hunting have outstanding results. Learn how to prospect. Today, it's not likely you are sitting on the phone "dialing for dollars" with the advent of so many social media tools and other resources.

Networking has not gone out of style. For many professional sales entrepreneurs, networking is a major and constant source of leads.

For the successful sales entrepreneur, success can be described as the freedom that exists from controlling your own schedule, the confidence in your own ability to perform, and the enjoyment of a significantly above-average income.

Lessons Learned:

▶ *Being a sales entrepreneur can create the freedom and independence you desire.*

▶ *Thoroughly research an industry and the company(ies) you plan to represent. Do your due diligence.*

▶ *Effective time management is more important than "the gift of gab."*

▶ *Try to choose an industry that facilitates the require-ment for repeat sales or residual income. If that's not possible, then you MUST have the ability to recruit oth-ers and derive an override; otherwise, you will always be limited to what you can accomplish yourself in a 40-hour week.*

▶ *Make sure you have a contract that explicitly lays out your compensation plan and limits any non-compete provisions.*

CHAPTER 11

NETWORK MARKETING

"If I had to do it all over again, rather than build an old-style type of business, I would have started building a network marketing business."

—*Robert T. Kiyosaki*
Entrepreneur
Author of "Rich Dad, Poor Dad" Book Series

I simply don't know a purer form of the free enterprise system (except possibly a lemonade stand!) than network marketing.

The potential for a person from any walk of life, level of education and socio-economic background to create a substantial income, freedom, financial independence and do it all without a large investment is what has made this industry continue to explode.

For those who have never been exposed to network marketing, here is a great definition from www.businessdictionary.com:

"(Network Marketing is a) Direct selling method in which independent agents serve as distributors of goods and services, and are encouraged to build and manage their own sales force by recruiting and training other independent agents. In this method, commission is earned on their own sales revenue, as well as on the sales revenue of the sales-force recruited by the agent and his or her recruits (called downline)."

I've had first-hand experience in this industry, building a large networking marketing organization that eventually supported my family and generated multi-million dollar annual cash flow.

Some call it a "poor man's franchise." Others ignorantly and erroneously refer to network marketing as a pyramid scheme. Make no mistake; these businesses have not only been historically mega-successful, but they are here to stay. There are new ones launched all the time.

Today, it's very hard to argue with the success of network marketing, multi-billion dollar industries with household names like Herbalife, NuSkin, Reliv, Amway and many others that have been listed on American stock exchanges and in other global stock exchanges.

Network marketing, or multi-level marketing, which began in 1941, is a legitimate, growing and accepted distribution model for all types of products and services. It's a great way to start a business with little capital, but the compensation potential is also serious enough to attract top professionals and existing business owners.

One of the main attractions of this type of business is the freedom and independence one can gain by building a successful network marketing business.

When I was first approached about joining a network marketing organization, I was near the end of my airfreight business career. Somewhat tired of the industry and looking for new challenges and opportunities, I joined one of the oldest and most traditional networking organizations in existence. Within two years, I had matched my airfreight business income without the hassle of employees, offices, forklifts, trucks, payroll and a ton of overhead.

This success allowed me the flexibility to sell my business.

There are many advantages to the network marketing business model. First, start-up costs are generally very low. Secondly, the education and training are typically outstanding, if you participate. Much like a franchise business, successful network marketing companies have developed training, marketing and systems for the distributor-entrepreneur to follow. There is no need to reinvent the wheel.

One thing typically missing in many businesses is the esprit de corps of the team or, in other words, everyone pulling for each other's success. In network marketing, your upline (those who have sponsored you into the business and their uplines) have a vested interest in your success, as you will in those who enter your downline. This fosters a symbiotic relationship where a person may strive to perform at a higher level because they are part of a team.

I spent $189 to buy a "starter kit" from a network marketing company in 1989, which gave me a few product samples and some collateral material. The next steps were to dive into the available training and personal development, which I could do at my own pace. Despite the fact that I had been in business for myself most of my adult life, I learned people skills and other techniques I would never have gotten otherwise except through this company's training, books, seminars and tapes.

Never underestimate the power of association. The old adage, "Steel sharpens steel," is not only preached but it is practiced in network marketing. Having the opportunity to learn from others who have gotten to a level I wanted to achieve was part of the formula that led to my success. In network marketing, you are constantly afforded these opportunities.

In my experience, there really is no competition within network marketing organizations with other distributors. The real competition is the general apathy of those who would rather live paycheck to paycheck and report to a cubicle every day.

In trying to find the right opportunity with a network marketing business, there are key fundamentals I look for that determine which one is best suited for what I would want to accomplish.

First and foremost, the company must be sound financially. If I'm going to spend precious hours of my life building a business and putting my reputation at stake by recruiting others, I need to know the company is rock solid.

Every multi-level organization will at some point face regulatory scrutiny, whether it is a state regulatory agency or federal. The Federal Trade Commission deemed these businesses legal as long as a product and service is actually sold to a consumer.

Network marketing distributors must make *retail sales* of some kind to non-distributors on a monthly or annual basis. If you are presented with an opportunity from a network marketing distributor, and all of the sales are driven by the self-consumption of the products or services by the distributor force — *run away fast!*

This requirement is what keeps a sales organization and network marketing from being a Ponzi or pyramid scheme.

When you understand this rule, you will look at the products and/or services offered in a different light. Are the products or services competitive? Many products and services offered by these companies are higher in price, but they typically offer some added benefits, ingredients or other superior quality over what one could buy at a discount store.

For you to be successful in this business, you must be your own best customer. Do you use the products? Can you vouch for the products and tell their story effectively to others?

Learn the differences in compensation plans, as there are approximately a half dozen or so generally accepted comp plans. If the products are great but the comp plan doesn't meet my requirements, then it is not a good fit and vice versa.

Generally speaking, this takes some study on the Internet to understand the subtle differences. I prefer comp plans in this industry to be binary plans for many reasons; structured properly, this type can have the most upside income potential.

When analyzing network marketing opportunities, make sure you study the top distributors, how long it took them to get where they are, how many people in their organization it takes to derive the income you're looking for, etc.

Most companies in this industry allow for differing levels of entry, from the most basic to the ability to "buy in" at a higher level when you begin. Be wary of any marketing plan where you are encouraged to spend thousands of dollars up front and load up on some type of inventory of the product or service.

Ideally, at the writing date of this book, you should be able to enter the highest level entry point at $1,500 or less. This is one area that gets the most attention from regulators and should be a warning sign to scrutinize closely. Where network marketing firms in the past have gotten into trouble, the upfront loading of products and services was the catalyst that could cause it to fail or get shut down. No heavy upfront loading of products and the ability and requirement to sell to end users outside of the distributor force are critically important to long-term viability.

There are few things more exciting in business than being on the ground floor of a young and exploding network marketing company. For me, I would make sure the ownership and management has had experience with another firm and knows what to expect. Experience in this area of the network marketing company is invaluable.

Would I build an organization with a network marketing firm that was not well established? Sure! But I would take extra effort to scrutinize the financial stability, the value of the products and, more important, the proven quality of the leadership of the organization.

Most of these organizations are closely held and do not publish their financial information. Here is where you have to be somewhat of a detective. I would start with checking the Better Business Bureau and the consumer complaints division of the attorney general's office in the state where the company is headquartered. See if your accountant or CPA can pull their Dunn & Bradstreet report.

Remember, if you are going to devote hours of your life to building this type of business, make sure to the best of your ability that the company will be there to pay you your just rewards as your organization grows.

Another important factor to consider is how the network marketing company reins in its distributor force when it comes to making money off their sales organizations. At issue with the network marketing company we associated with was the refusal by the network marketing company to monitor, control and regulate the larger distributors who had created another significant income stream from the sale of tapes, books and seminars to their downline to the detriment of the core product line. In fact, it had gotten to the point where the money made from these outside sources was more significant than the payouts from the company's comp plan.

This became such a large issue that we eventually sold our distributorship and sued the network marketing company, vindicated by a large settlement years later.

Since this was really a business inside a business, it didn't catch my closer scrutiny early on until I had a significant cash flow.

Network marketing companies should operate like franchises, wherein they (like the franchisor) control the marketing message. The sale of any collateral materials, tapes, books and functions should be completely controlled and produced by the network marketing company, not the distributors. Allowing the independent sale of these materials by distributors to other distributors would be a giant red flag to me when considering a network marketing opportunity.

Another caution is if the company is producing health and wellness products. A network marketing company can get into trouble with the Food and Drug Administration (FDA) with unverified health claims. The health and wellness category is probably the largest category of offerings in the network marketing industry. For this reason, do your research on FDA complaints and active state attorney general lawsuits against any potential network marketing company.

When I started making several thousand dollars a month, I started to carry my monthly checks around to show them to prospects. It made perfect sense to me. I probably would have gotten involved sooner had someone showed me his or her monthly check. The problem with that approach is that the Federal Trade Commission (FTC) prohibits it, as it can be seen as an improper inducement. Their theory is that one person's success is not necessarily indicative of others and it offers no guarantees.

Leave it to the federal government to create a law or regulatory rule for what should be obvious to anyone.

Many network marketing companies have their own cultures, just like any other large enterprise. I have found that the cultural differences of network marketing companies can be vastly different. Some of those cultures simply do not work for me and may not for you. This is really true of any business opportunity, including franchises. Make sure you can see yourself fitting into any particular culture on a long-term basis.

It is possible that network marketing provides the largest potential with the lowest start-up costs for any business venture. In business, this is typically called return on investment (ROI). I call it the *Renegade Capitalist® Quotient*. The formula works like this:

(Start-up Costs + Overhead + Effort) X Residual Factor/ Time = *Renegade Capitalist® Quotient*

Network marketing offers the important requirements of the *Renegade Capitalist®* such as low start-up costs, training, growth potential, part-time capability, duplicity and residual income.

Do your research. Go to some opportunity meetings and, if this is your chosen path, get started!

Lessons Learned:

▶ *Network marketing is a proven business concept.*

▶ *Few business models offer the income potential and freedom that successful network marketers enjoy.*

▶ *Do your due diligence on network marketing companies for regulatory issues, distributor lawsuits and product claims.*

▶ *Attend some network marketing meetings to get a feel for the distributors involved and the culture.*

▶ *Avoid network marketing companies that want to "front load" you with products or services.*

▶ *Run from network marketing companies that allow their distributors to create their own marketing materials, especially those distributors that derive an income from selling self-produced training materials and seminars.*

Chapter 12

Should I Buy a Franchise?

*"If you want to become a franchisee, you have to lose your ego.
Even if you come to the table with 25 years of experience as
a VP of operations and you know more than the franchisor."*

—Joel Libava
a.k.a. "The Franchise King"®
Author and Entrepreneur

Rarely does a day go by that you don't spend a dollar or more at some kind of franchise. From buying your lunch, to pumping gas into your vehicle, to buying a new pair of jeans, the list is endless. You probably never considered the fact that you were spending your money at a franchise.

Franchising has become a super-successful model worldwide and incorporates every industry conceivable. Most people think of McDonalds® as the most recognizable franchise concept in history.

The actual concept of franchising goes way back in history. I like to think of the Catholic Church as one of the originators of the franchise concept, although not for the same reason you or I would think of starting a franchise.

As the Church sent missionaries across the globe, and when churches were established by those missionaries and had parishioners tithing to their local churches, a portion of those contributions always went back to the Vatican. This funded missionary expeditions and supported churches in poorer areas, Catholic hospitals and Church administration. It was a very successful model of growth with a greater purpose in mind.

The majority of tithed funds go to the local church, local outreach missions and the rest to the diocese (regional authority) and then to the Vatican.

Many of today's franchises have a similar structure where the majority of revenue is kept by the franchisee, with a percentage paid to the master franchisee (someone who may have paid the franchisor an amount to own the rights to a specific region) and then another percentage to the franchisor.

Apart from starting a new business from scratch, what someone is really purchasing when they buy a proven franchise is a "system" for generating profits. Most of the kinks have already been worked out and the franchise owner does not have to reinvent the wheel as opposed to a startup, where everything must be designed, built and developed somewhere along the way.

An important advantage of the franchise model is the support system that helps franchisees with everything from marketing to accounting to business processes.

There is almost every type of franchise for just about any industry. Also, there are very inexpensive franchises to very capital-intensive franchises. A McDonald's franchise, for example, is a very capital-intensive investment, whereas a janitorial franchise entry fee can be as little as a month's salary or less.

The way a franchise works is that a prospective franchisee pays a one-time fee for the rights to a certain territory, plus a percentage of revenue or profits for a contracted amount of time. In exchange, you get the franchisor's help establishing the business, training on how to run it, location advice, marketing support, use of the name and logo, and other administrative functions. The level of support between franchises can vary greatly.

One mistake many new franchise owners make is that they make an investment and sometimes believe that automatically should result in revenue. Even a franchise with a proven concept has to find customers.

I owned a franchise in the airfreight industry for several years. Like any other franchise, it had its advantages and disadvantages. Here are a few common advantages to going the franchise route for going into business for yourself:

1. Proven business model/established processes

2. Training

3. Typically, marketing support of some kind

4. Experience of the franchisor and other successful franchisees

5. No need to reinvent the wheel

6. Already established trade vendor accounts

Here are a few disadvantages:

1. Entry costs can sometimes be astronomical. If you're trying to replace a large corporate income, it is harder to do right away without a large investment in a capital-intensive franchise model or without multiple franchise units.

2. Franchises are typically very restrictive on how the

franchisee operates. There won't be much, if any, room for your own creativity in any facet of the operation.

3. Not ideal for the person who needs to start part-time or bootstrap a business because of their current financial condition unless your spouse or other family members can run it while you work your regular job.

4. Most franchise royalties are based on "gross" revenues. I prefer ones based on net profit; however, I concede that most franchise models require the gross revenue model. The royalties I paid in my airfreight franchise were on "net" profits. It is very important to pay attention to what current franchisees experience in net profits when the franchisor is taking royalties from gross revenue.

5. Be wary of certain retail-based franchises, as you may essentially be exchanging one job for another with a lot more liabilities. Most retail franchises in the food industry, for example, are much too hard to run as a manager model, where the owner doesn't have to be there eighty hours a week!

6. Many franchisors have very strict limits on your exit strategy or ability to sell your franchise to whomever you like or whenever you like.

7. Be very leery of non-compete language as a part of your contract. Get legal advice.

8. Your ability to offer products or services to customers that complement those products and services offered by the franchisor may be completely restricted, resulting in an inability to expand your revenue outside of the current franchise model.

Do your homework! Many larger cities have franchise opportunity shows that come to major convention centers, sometimes twice per year. At these shows, hundreds of franchises have booths, demonstrations and information on their franchise concepts.

For any franchise you are considering, it is absolutely imperative before signing any franchise agreement to take the following steps:

Ask the franchisor for contact information from existing franchise owners. Ask for dozens — and call EVERY single one of them. By the time you get done talking to existing franchise owners, you will get a feel for whether the business is right for you, and whether the franchisor has integrity. If the franchisor refuses to provide names and contact information, run away, very fast! Also ask the franchisor for *dissatisfied* franchisees. All franchises have them. If they say they don't or won't supply their contact information, be very leery of the franchise.

Read the *entire* franchise memorandum and agreement, redline any notes, and then take these documents to the experts — a qualified attorney and a CPA. Any money spent on these professionals is well worth it.

Go online and check the Better Business Bureau for both customer experiences with the franchise, but also check for complaints by their own franchisees. Check your local state attorney general's office for complaints, and make sure to check the home state in which the franchise has its corporate headquarters.

Ask them specifically whether they are in any lawsuits with franchisees or customers, and get the details. Most lawsuits are public record. Go online and read the pleadings.

Lessons Learned:

▶ *Franchises are a great way to go into business for yourself with many advantages, primarily a proven business model, training and marketing assistance.*

▶ *Go to franchise opportunity shows to learn what franchises interest you.*

▶ *Read the franchise memorandum thoroughly and get professional accounting and legal advice before investing.*

▶ *Do your homework and due diligence up front.*

▶ *Make sure you understand the cash flow of the business. Many new franchise owners underestimate how long it will take to replace their current income. Note: It's always at least twice as long as you think.*

▶ *Understand the limitations for creativity, introduction of other revenue streams and any non-compete restrictions.*

▶ *Franchise opportunities run the gamut of products, services and industries. Make sure you choose an industry that you would enjoy long-term.*

▶ *Be wary of retail franchises, as those typically require you to open for business seven days a week. You may long to have your old forty hours-per-week job back...*

CHAPTER 13

DO I REALLY NEED A BUSINESS PLAN?

"Anyone will buy something once. Your goal as a small business owner is to provide an outstanding customer experience to get your consumers to buy over and over again from you."

—*Melinda F. Emerson*
Author and Entrepreneur
Named to Forbes® Top 20 Women
for Entrepreneurs to Follow

The simple answer is "yes."

Before you ever get started on a business plan, it's important to figure out your *life plan*. Starting a business is going to alter your life in so many ways that it's vital to know the end game you have in mind.

Is it more freedom? More money? Respect? Control?

Of course, it's probably all of those. When I was twenty-one years old writing my three-page business plan for our airfreight business, I couldn't see five or ten years down the road. All I knew was I had to get it done and I needed to be in business. I couldn't stand one more day in the chains of employment!

I wish I could find the original business plan. My guess is that it was based on short-term goals which, for me and where I was in life at that very moment, was enough to get me started.

If you buy a franchise, the franchisor will provide this to you based on their proven track record, which can be semi-customized to fit your particular market and niche.

Network marketing companies will also have a proven plan to follow.

But, if you are going to start what we will consider a traditional business, a business plan is an absolute necessity. In fact, if you are planning to borrow money from a bank or institution to start a business, not only will you have to have a business plan, but an accompanying pro forma (anticipated financial statements, profit and loss, financial projections, etc.). I highly recommend a business plan also be produced for anyone who may lend you money for your venture or invest in it, such as family and friends (more on this in a later chapter).

If you are vacillating back and forth and playing with the idea of being in business for yourself, this exercise for your life plan is more important. Starting a business almost always involves sacrifices. You may work more hours. You may see your family less at first. You may miss out on the next gadget. You may still perceive yourself as risk-averse. For those with hesitations, some soul searching is in order. It's normal to have hesitations, but hesitation can lead to inaction, which may later result in regret and missed opportunities.

Knowing your life plan will help you with your financial commitment to your business, too. In other words, how much of your current financial position are you willing to alter (and thus your lifestyle) to get where you want to go and change your lifestyle forever?

If you're married, does your spouse know your goals? Is your spouse on board and willing to make the same sacrifices if necessary? Are all members of the team pulling in the same direction?

I've seen many, many dreams die at the hands of a spouse who killed the dream in their partner because they had a flawed idea of what real security looks like.

Here's a clue; it's not a job!

There are tons of available online business plan templates and software. Find one of these that works for you. Unless you are seeking angel investors or a bank loan, simpler is better. For simplicity's sake, these should be the major components of your business plan:

1. Summary description of the business (Elevator Pitch/ Business Concept)

2. Detailed description of the business

3. Start-up plan including details on how you will finance your startup and what you would consider significant milestones to measure progress

4. Marketing details (who are your customers and how do you find them and ultimately keep them)

5. Financial details, including pro forma financial projections

If you are an entrepreneur who decides to step off and leave full-time employment in your new venture, it is critical that a business plan be formalized so you can plan **NOT** to run out of money.

So many ventures fail because the owners didn't project their cash flow properly and the *burn rate* (negative monthly cash-flow)

was unsustainable. How many of these failed businesses were just weeks or months from turning the corner? We'll never know, but I can guarantee, if the concept was sound, they either never figured out how to drive customers or didn't manage their cash. However, there is no amount of cash that will spring a dead idea to life.

How do you know if your idea will work? Ask someone, particularly someone who would use or buy your product or service. I had the benefit of starting businesses in industries I became familiar with in short periods of time.

If someone asked me to open a florist shop, used car lot or hotel, I would have to do my homework. Most business concepts are universal, but I would have to study their cash flow, capital investment costs, return on investment and how they get customers, etc.

The most critical piece of this part of the planning process is a realistic understanding of the cash necessary to operate. For this reason, if cash is tight, many businesses are simply better to start part-time if possible.

For those willing to risk their life savings, or borrow money from a bank, family or investor, the business plan creation process needs to be well thought out. After all, in these scenarios, there is a lot at stake.

All of this being said, I can honestly say that not one business plan I developed into a successful business remotely resembled the original business plan three years later. This is because there will be mistakes in your business plan, changes in the economy, new opportunities recognized and unforeseen events.

A business plan should be a living, breathing document that describes your business model, but one that can be adjusted along the way. In several of my businesses, if I hadn't been flexible enough to make slight or even major changes along the way, the businesses never would have survived. That doesn't mean that if you have an idea that you are absolutely sold out to that you should abandon it at the first sign of rough waters. The key here is to be able to recognize the difference between the day-to-day challenges of running a business versus a flawed model. I can tell you it's not an exact science, but more of an art.

I'm not a pilot but, on a recent flight on one of our corporate aircraft, I watched the pilot continually adjusting the trim, altitude, etc. to keep the same heading. It reminded me of the life of a business. The business environment around you will, in fact, continue to change but, if you know where you are headed, you can make the necessary changes on the fly and still get there. Weather, headwinds and air traffic may make you adjust your flight path, but the destination is always the goal.

My business plans have ranged from a simple one-page outline to a very technical business plan and pro forma (future estimate) that we used to raise $3.6 million for Teligistics in a formal private offering memorandum.

Even if your goal is to have a one-person business, you need a compass or plan, but it doesn't have to be complex or one hundred pages long.

Many times I have had people bring me their business plans to evaluate, invest in or critique. In the majority of these cases, the prospective entrepreneur cannot state in concise terms *exactly* what the proposed business is, much less how it will get customers, or how it compares to the current market.

During the road show we did to present our private offering to potential investors for Teligistics, I presented to a room full of institutional investors, venture capitalists and angel investors at The Yale Club® in New York City.

This event was during the dot.com days when business plans were being assigned astronomical valuations (worth) with absolutely no existing revenue or proven concepts. There were twenty or so prospective companies presenting over two days. The company that presented right before we did was an online greeting card company startup.

I'm not an expert on all subject matter, but I know a little bit about business. I sat through their thirty-minute presentation and I swear to this day I cannot tell you how that business was going to make money or have a sustainable business model. If I could sit in that room and not see the potential, I guarantee the venture capitalists didn't either.

The first rule of any business plan should be the same as the famous business investment vernacular known as *the elevator pitch.* The elevator pitch is based on the premise that you should be able to state in brief and concise terms exactly what your business does on the short ride of an elevator — likely less than twenty seconds. If you use this concept for your business plan, especially in the beginning description, you will go a long way to crystallizing your focus, and anyone who sees your business plan will understand what your business is and how it will work.

Here's an example of the Teligistics elevator pitch today:

"What does Teligistics do?"

My reply: "Teligistics acts as an outsourced telecom department for large global enterprises, using proprietary technology solutions to source these services strategically, reduce costs, and provide financial management and visibility."

Lessons Learned:

▶ *A business plan helps you organize your thoughts and plans for your business.*

▶ *Every business should have a business plan.*

▶ *Your business plan will likely morph over time with changing business conditions, unforeseen events and new opportunities.*

▶ *A formal business plan with pro forma financials is always necessary if you are borrowing money or taking investment from others into your business equity.*

▶ *Practice exactly what you will say to someone when they ask about your business. Know your elevator pitch backward and forward. If you get confused looks when you give your pitch, you probably need to modify it. Try it out on others and continue to improve it.*

▶ *Use the countless tools available online to lay out your business plan.*

▶ *Just because a business plan is professional-looking doesn't mean the underlying business is viable. Do your market research, especially with potential customers.*

CHAPTER 14

A BUCKET FULL OF CRABS AND THE INFINITE GUNSLINGER

"It's hard to beat a person who never gives up!"

—*Babe Ruth*
Major League Baseball Hall of Famer

Throughout my life I've had doubters. You will, too.

I was too young to start an airfreight business.

I had no capital and never ran my own company.

I never worked for a telecommunications company.

I never raised money from angel investors.

Heck, if I had listened to all the doubters, procrastinators, hecklers and those jealous of my ambitions, I probably would be working in some dead-end government or union job.

While I was in the network marketing business, I heard someone describe the *Crab Theory* to us at an event. I had never heard of this before, so the next time I went fishing in the Gulf, I tested the theory.

I bought about ten live blue crabs and put them in a large bucket. Every time one of the crabs tried to free itself from the bucket and got close to the top and thereby close to gaining freedom, the other crabs underneath them who were also trying to get out pulled down the crab at the top of the heap! The *Crab Theory* was true. Every once in while a crab was able to escape, but it was rare.

I already knew this was true with humans in life, but it was fun to see where the theory originated.

Let's face facts here. Other than your family and close friends, who else wants to see you succeed or, for that matter, who really cares? You may think this is a pessimistic way of looking at life and society, but I've seen it too many times to ignore.

Unfortunately, some of us even have so-called friends and family members who secretly — or outwardly — don't want us to succeed. In fact, one of the most significant issues I dealt with in my network marketing business was the fact that so many spouses had no belief in their partners, or even wanted them to try to break out of the bucket! This hit me like a brick in the face.

Since my wonderful wife has always been supportive, to the point where we literally ate beans while I was on one of the *down cycles* of my entrepreneurial exploits, I never could understand the negativity of a non-supportive spouse. I am literally blessed that my wife never *commanded* me to go get a *secure job* (oxymoron). She believed in me, and has been rewarded for that faith.

I have seen people literally become emotional, their face light up and have hope that they have finally found an avenue to break out of a paltry existence living paycheck to paycheck, only to have their spouses literally dash their hopes and dreams, and many times in a hateful manner.

Don't think this has been limited to the wife. I've seen many men shrink from the idea that it's time to put on their big boy britches, step up to the plate and do what is necessary for them to provide for their families.

I've seen it demonstrated in many and various subtle ways.

It's the overly analytical types who, when presented with absolute logic, get *analysis paralysis*, unable to act because their own fears trump the path in front of them that leads them out of the bucket forever.

The same guy who wouldn't invest $500 in himself to start a business that may take him out of his comfort zone will spend thousands of dollars on a vacation he puts on his credit cards, thousands of dollars on cigarettes or a new lifestyle purchase that he can't afford to begin with.

I just love the guy or gal who makes sure they point out the character flaws, weaknesses and why-nots of their life partner with statements like, "Well, Jim just isn't a people person," or "Mary wouldn't be any good at that…" and, many times, this is said right in front of their partner!

I am a living, breathing example of the saying that for every successful person there is a "good woman" or "good man" behind them.

I truly never understood the dynamics of many relationships that would cause a person to remain with a partner who had no belief in them, or to remain with someone they don't believe in.

I'm no marriage or relationship counselor, but it would seem in these scenarios some professional counseling is in order.

Life is awfully short to deal with negative people, *especially* when they are negative about *your* dreams! Your partner shouldn't be the most negative person in your life.

I really do believe the environment and association you have with negative people will rub off on you. Have you ever caught yourself having a conversation with one or more people and the conversation goes downhill quickly with everyone complaining about someone or something? These are the conversations to walk away from. They drain your energy and drive.

What I'm about to tell you is harsh. I know that.

Simply put, you have to avoid negative people in your life — like the plague! I'm serious. You don't want to catch what they have!

When I get around negative people, I literally want to run.

The old adage that states, "Advice not asked for is not well received," should be your motto. In the next chapter we will discuss *where* to get that advice.

If you are asking me, "Should I avoid family if they are negative and want to tear down my dreams and ambitions for being self-employed or any other dream I have?" — simply, yes.

That doesn't mean you shouldn't love them nor should you treat them with disrespect. Just consider them to have a contagious disease (chronic negativity) and love them from afar!

I have a simple rule that I figured out years ago with some of my family members.

If I feel worse about my ideas, my ambitions or myself after speaking with them, they are infected, and the sooner I can be decontaminated the better!

Not everyone deals with rejection or criticism the same way. For many years I internalized these negative emotions caused by others.

When I picked up a phone to call an executive who I never met, who was older than I was, or held some business title I thought was important, I was terrified.

As a kid, I was just as happy to play by myself and could provide my own entertainment in just about any environment. If I didn't want to talk to anyone I didn't have to.

In business, and to reach my dreams, I had to talk to people. You will, too. It may not be in a traditional sales role, but you will have to talk to people, whether it's your customers, vendors or employees.

It took me about six to eight months when I was in network marketing to finally get comfortable being in a stranger's home. If I could meet someone over lunch or at a coffee shop as opposed to being in their home, I would go out of my way to make that happen.

What causes someone to get out of their comfort zone and to finally do the things necessary to grow their business?

For me, it was fear. Fear of failure. My fear of failing was greater than my fear of not succeeding. Yes, I wanted all the nice things for me and my family that being successful would provide. I also loved any recognition that came my way. Many times people are driven by the respect they achieve or the special recognition that may be laid upon them.

Just like there was a turning point for me in college that shaped the direction of my life, so was there too in business. Faced with a business downturn we neither planned for nor embraced, my brother and I squabbled and eventually split in our first airfreight venture. Generally, he had run sales and was very good at it while I ran the operations. Both of those areas performed at a very high level, leading to massive early success at a young age.

Because of our financial illiteracy, business planning and listening to bad advice (our own fault), we ultimately failed. Not only did we fail, but my brother and I went separate ways (didn't speak for years). To add to the venom, we both stayed in the same industry and competed for the same customers!

My brother landed on his feet right away with another sales gig with a competitor and got a sign-on bonus to boot! Me? I scrambled and put together another airfreight business, but now I *had* to learn how to sell.

I hate to lose. I mean I really, really hate to lose. Do you?

I literally got angry. This was one of the *eating beans* periods of our lives.

It's funny how many business successes come from a bad break, a terrible event or a troubling time. This was a terrible time for us. I had to put food on the table for my wife and kids.

I woke up every day with a purpose. Rejections? Go ahead and give me your best shot!

I believed in the processes I put in place for our airfreight operations and I carried them over to the new enterprise. We did a great job for our clients and I knew it.

I developed this picture in my mind whenever someone hurt me, rejected my ideas or me, or criticized my business. These moments were "bullets" I put in my belt holster, just like gunfighters in the 1880s.

These criticisms and rejections eventually gave me a ton of firepower. To this day, someone cannot give me a logical argument why they won't use our products or services in one of our businesses. I got to the point where I can shoot down any argument or reasonable objection.

When you believe that much in your business, concept or idea, you will be the same. At some point, you stop hearing the rejections and unsolicited criticisms because they are either petty or come from those uninformed or whose opinions don't matter.

The great news is that I never run out of bullets! I have an uninterrupted supply of ammo; therefore, I am the infinite gunslinger!

You will be, too!

Lessons Learned:

- ▶ *Avoid negative people at all costs — the Crab Theory.*

- ▶ *Business is hard. It's challenging. It's even more challenging with an unsupportive spouse or partner. Some serious introspection on a relationship may be necessary prior to embarking on a business if the dream of the business is only owned by one, but not the other.*

- ▶ *Associate with those who support your business, ideas, concepts and ambitions.*

- ▶ *The more sold out you are to your business idea, the easier it will be to overcome rejection and criticism.*

- ▶ *Sometimes life's calamities can be blessings in disguise. Embrace them, learn from them, and let them motivate you!*

- ▶ *Find what motivates you. Hint: It may not be money — and that's okay!*

CHAPTER 15

THE GREAT UN-PACKING

"Is there anyone so wise as those who have learned from the experience of others?"

—*Voltaire*
French Philosopher and Author

S everal years ago, I was fortunate enough to get invited by a good friend to go hunting on an exclusive Texas ranch owned by a man who was at the time ranked as one of the richest men in America.

We arrived early on a Friday afternoon at his huge spread that was adorned by exotic game, longhorn cattle and a beautiful ranch house and guest cabins. The ranch had its own chef and, after a great dinner and conversation, we settled into the ranch parlor for drinks and a cigar. The parlor was decorated with wildlife game mounts from all over the world.

There were eight of us scheduled to go on a quail and pheasant hunt and we were to get up around 5:30 in the morning.

At about ten o'clock the night before, tired from travel and belly full from a fantastic meal, fine wine and single malt scotch whiskey, everyone seemed to be turning in for the night.

Our host, the multi-billionaire who at the time was every bit of eighty years old, poured another glass of wine for himself as folks were going to bed. I pulled up a barstool right next to his, and on the other side of him was my Teligistics co-founder and business partner, Randy Councill.

Since it was just the three of us, we began asking him very specific business questions. We were literally *unpacking* his business brain!

We learned how he started his business driving a truck and how he was given an opportunity to own a piece of a gas and oil pipeline for doing work on the pipeline without pay but for a future interest in the pipeline. This man went on to become the largest owner of natural gas and oil pipelines in America.

There were many fascinating stories and tidbits that he shared with us that night. One thing that was amazing was that he really seemed to enjoy the depth of the questions we asked. Conversation about finance, employees, customers, vendors and politics flowed as freely as the wine and scotch.

He admitted even his own children and employees had never asked him the pointed and detailed questions we posed.

In my mind, I was sitting there with a self-made multi-billionaire! I was not going to waste an opportunity to pick the brain of someone with so much success and experience.

I could not believe the others went to bed. Some, but not all of them, were business owners themselves. When else in their lives was an opportunity like that going to be presented to them?

It was an incredible night that didn't end until well after 3:00

a.m., despite the fact that we were all to get up in just a couple of short hours for our first hunt.

In the previous chapter, I discussed avoiding or associating with negative people and how such an environment can be detrimental to your goals.

Well, the opposite is also true.

I heard somewhere that, if you want what someone else has, whether it be their lifestyle or money, you need to learn to do what they did.

In other words, you need a mentor, or mentors.

The least expensive, but ironically the most powerful education you can ever give yourself, is to learn from others' mistakes, failures and successes.

Learn to associate with people who have the success in life you want, whatever that might be.

Why, for instance, would someone go ask someone who has never started a business, never achieved success in business, never made a payroll or done anything else in life but worked a job their opinion on a business, unless they viewed that person as a potential customer?

This would be like asking my college economics professor at what point in my business do I hire my first employee?

I think many people would be surprised at how willing most business owners and entrepreneurs are willing to share their experiences. Once they size you up and decide you aren't going to compete with them directly, they are generally willing to open up and help you.

Look closely at those around you in your everyday life. I would bet you may have a family member, neighbor, fellow church member or business associate who is either a business owner or knows one they can introduce you to.

One advantage franchises and network marketing professionals have is a ready-made cadre of like-minded people to associate with. The franchisor and other successful franchisees can serve as mentors to the budding franchisees. Likewise, successful distributors and the parent organization have a vested interest in your success in network marketing.

If you are on your own, it's important to find these mentors. Find others who are top performers in your chosen industry. Go to conventions and association meetings where these owners congregate.

There is another old saying, "Steel sharpens steel!"

Associating with others who have a positive attitude and the same general goals, values and ambitions will sharpen you!

Lessons Learned:

▶ *Seek out people who have what you want!*

▶ *Learn to associate with positive people and those who have similar interests, goals and ambitions.*

▶ *Never pass up the opportunity to "un-pack" a successful person's ideas on business and success.*

▶ *Find mentors in business and in life!*

CHAPTER 16

BOOTSTRAPPING TO SUCCESS

"Bootstrapping is a way to do something about the problems you have without letting someone else give you permission to do them."

—*Tom Warner*
Co-Founder of GitHub

"Sweat equity is the best startup capital."

—*Mark Cuban*
Billionaire owner of the Dallas Mavericks
Co-founder of Broadcast.com
Founder of HDNet

Of all the businesses I have started, there wasn't a single one where I plopped down a bunch of cash to get if off the ground. Later, and after we had revenue and some profit, we did a formal raise of serious capital for Teligistics but, as stated in an earlier chapter, Teligistics was initially started with $1,000.

However, it has never been lost on me that there was a time when I couldn't scrape together $1,000 if my life depended on it. The principal reason was because I was financially illiterate. Those who, like me, could be completely derailed by an unexpected refrigerator or car repair either have an income problem or an expense problem and, more often than not, it's both.

Bootstrapping a business is probably the number one method for how people go into business for themselves. Businesses that start this way generally don't use external money from investors, bank loans, etc. in the early stages. Typically, if you bootstrap, you are using our own money and, more often than not, it's not a tremendous amount of money.

Part of the bootstrapping process is an extreme focus to keep expenses low during the start-up phase and making sure cash flow is positive. In a bootstrapping model, getting to profitability is a race to not run out of cash.

When we were doing our roadshow for our private offering, I would be amazed to hear other entrepreneurs almost bragging about their *burn rate* (negative cash flow associated with losing money on a monthly basis). What surprised me was the number of months or, in some cases, years they would accept a burn rate at all. Unfortunately, it's always easier to burn through cash when it's someone else's cash. An entrepreneur who is bootstrapping does not have that luxury.

This is where some of the lessons learned in the earlier chapter on financial literacy really pay dividends.

First of all, if you have kept your living expenses low and have been living on less than you make, then you likely have a modest savings account that can be used to fund at least some of the expenses of a startup. If not, you will have to make every dollar stretch because, when you don't have money put away and are living paycheck to paycheck, putting money out for business expenses typically means some other household bill likely isn't getting paid.

While in bootstrapping mode, monies that are spent need to prioritized. Even if you don't know what business you are considering starting, there are a few principles for bootstrapping that are worth emphasizing.

First and foremost, provided you have done your homework and are convinced you have a market for your product or service, all the focus for your funds should be on getting the product or service to market. That means that, if you have a product and you need a website to sell the product, get the website built. If you have a prototype product and need to produce samples, get it done. Again, I cannot stress enough that you should already have done some research, even if it is just asking people you know if they would buy your product and/or service. Hopefully you asked some people who would give you some honest feedback.

Not that your mother isn't honest, but moms sometimes get caught up in the excitement and enthusiasm you have for your idea and the belief her son/daughter would surely be a success at anything they tried!

So many times I see fledgling business owners spending their limited resources on items that aren't going to result in revenue. A perfect example is someone I know who spent $5,000 on a massive desk and credenza set-up for the office he put in his home, despite the fact that his product needed more development and that he was going to need to spend some money to get it marketed.

Check out crowd-funding sites such as Kickstarter.com. Crowd-funding sites are unique ways to raise money for your company, typically without giving up any equity ownership. If you can be creative in your approach, this is a fantastic way to raise early funds.

As mentioned earlier, we started Teligistics with two folding metal chairs (one was bent) and a folding card table (that didn't match the chairs). That set-up wouldn't have impressed a potential client if we had been starting a new law firm or needed to have an acceptable place to receive customers. Tailor your bootstrapping decisions to what is important to get paying customers. Even if we had to have a place to meet customers, it wouldn't have been a high rent space with new furniture.

Be very careful about using credit cards. I never had the luxury of using any credit lines for my early startups because I had none. This was probably by divine intervention, because the level of my financial illiteracy was at a point where I probably would have created a lot of debt at unsustainable interest rates.

In my opinion, the use of credit cards for startups is dangerous, although there are plenty of examples where a business owner used credit cards to purchase pre-sold inventory, etc. My best advice regarding the use of credit cards is that it's helpful to have them in an emergency, but relying on them is extremely risky if you aren't financially literate and disciplined. Filling a purchase order may be an acceptable use of a credit card while bootstrapping, but pay it off when the customers pay.

For the bootstrapping entrepreneur, it's almost as important for you to find less expensive methods of operating as it is for you to generate revenue. Get good at finding deals on the items you may need.

There is nothing wrong with buying good used equipment. There is also nothing wrong with finding an up-to-date designer suit in a second-hand clothing store. Be smart where you spend your money. For every dollar you spend on general expenses, it's a dollar that can't be used to create other dollars by finding customers or developing your product or services.

Here is another area where your mentor(s) can help. Find out where they buy their supplies, furniture, computers, etc.

A bootstrapping entrepreneur can also go to the opposite extreme in this area, too. The business owner who uses ten gallons of gas and causes wear and tear on his or her vehicle to drive across town to save $75 on an item they need for the business is probably penny wise but dollar foolish.

In that same amount of time, how many new customers or sales could have been made? How about that new product design that needed a couple more hours to finish? Focus on the important things and manage the little things as you have time.

Make sure you aren't throwing dollars away to gain pennies.

Lessons Learned:

► *Bootstrapping is an efficient way to do a start-up business when capital is lacking.*

► *When money is tight, use what you have to advance the product and revenue. Everything else is secondary.*

► *Unless you become financially literate, bootstrapping will probably be a foreign concept to you.*

► *Avoid using credit cards to finance your startup.*

► *Sell things you don't need or use to help with start-up costs.*

► *Consider used equipment instead of new.*

► *Tap your mentor(s) for advice in these areas.*

CHAPTER 17

WHERE'S MY ANGEL? — THE PRIVATE OFFERING

"If you don't have savings, and your co-founders are as poor as you are and, if Mom and Dad won't loan you money, then your best bet is to find people that know you — your friends. If they, too, won't help, then you're stuck seeking out angel investors."

—*Vivek Wadhwa*
American Technology Entrepreneur & Academic

I won't kid you… raising money for a business is a very tough prospect — doable, but tough.

The first question to ask yourself is whether you want any other partners, investors or shareholders involved in your business.

The very minute you take investment money from others, you are beholden to them for any and all actions you take with your business. There are fiduciary responsibilities and potential liabilities, including the likelihood of required annually audited financials (expensive), annual shareholders' meetings and a board of directors.

Personally, I would never consider investment by others in my entities unless I had enough control of the company's shares to effectively manage the enterprise. It is entirely possible for an elected board of directors to fire the entrepreneur once there are enough controlling shares of stock on the board that don't belong to the original entrepreneur. There are thousands of horror stories of this exact scenario, and some of them are from very high profile successful organizations.

You will have to balance the potential value investors bring to the table. Personally, I prefer investors who can bring more than just money to the table, such as specific expertise, experience and connections.

There are essentially two types of money that get invested into businesses — debt or equity.

Debt is a loan. Equity is giving up a percentage of your ownership in exchange for money. Many times, private investment into businesses can be a combination of both and can get very complex.

There are institutional investors and there are angel investors. The difference between them is an institutional investment generally comes from a venture capital firm, an investment division of a large bank, or a private equity firm. Institutional investors also usually require a place on your board of directors and can be involved in the day-to-day operations of your business.

Angel investors can be anyone from your rich uncle to private individuals who have available capital for investment into businesses.

There are a myriad of methods for raising capital for a business depending on your type of business, the industry and what your goals are. For instance, raising money from angel investors or from a venture capital firm is significantly simpler if you already have revenue, and you stand a better chance of generating interest and ultimately a deal if you have profits.

There are also benefits to buying an existing business that already has revenue and profits, but these deals generally can require more capital and the absolute necessity to perform the proper due diligence (discussed in a later chapter).

Based on my experiences, the general rule of thumb is that an investor looks for more than an average return he or she can get in the stock market or a bank certificate of deposit. Most experienced and sophisticated investors want a minimum of a 20 percent or more return within five years or less. This is because the risk of investment is much higher than a savings account. If the venture is deemed riskier than normal, the angel investor will want a higher return in exchange for the risk.

Interesting dynamics start to take shape when you take an investment with other people's money and, when it's family that invests, you add another potential dynamic that can include drama and conflict.

Just as in any other investments, an equity or debt investment (a loan) from a family member should be treated just the same as if it was an institutional investor. Your angel investor should have seen a business plan, had plenty of opportunities to ask questions and, if necessary, have signed a mutual confidentiality and non-disclosure document. In the event they invest, a written contract document is *absolutely* necessary.

The document should state the terms of the deal, payback schedule (if debt), equity ownership (if applicable) and a definitive statement that the investors or loaners know they may lose their entire investment.

This is an area where you need to consult a qualified attorney. Do not take money from any angel, even if it is family, without documenting the terms.

There are too many stories of families that have split up over issues with lending or investing money into another family member's business or venture. The business doesn't have to be a failure for serious fissures in family relationships to occur. Even family members who have invested in a business from a fellow family member whose business is a rousing success can create a different dynamic, causing stress, drama and conflict.

Get the terms of the deal in a valid and legal document. Don't put it off until later, no matter how close a family member might be or what you think that person can afford to lose.

Many times, angel investors feel more comfortable with investments into something tangible in which there is a proven track record, such as a franchise or the purchase of an ongoing business.

As our growth at Teligistics was very fast, we reached a point where, in order to sustain growth, we needed additional capital. Most of our costs were involved in software development and marketing. These are two areas where banks don't lend money without collateralizing the loan with hard assets. For us, an equity investment by either institutional or angel investors was a better choice.

We raised $3.56 million dollars over about a year through what is called a private offering memorandum. This is also called a Section 504(D) offering because it is covered in that particular section of Securities and Exchange Commission (SEC) regulations.

This type of private offering of equity shares of your company requires professional assistance. Do not try to do this on your own.

Doing a private offering without a ready-made list of angel

investors to present the offering to is also a mistake. Just because someone has a private offering available does not mean angel investors will flock to it to invest.

A private offering has to be marketed. It also has a spoil rate. The longer it is opened, the less attractive to investors it becomes. Because of that it is important that the offer is not for too much money. Better to close out a smaller private offering round because it was funded quickly than one that languishes as it will scare off investors.

You should get an honest assessment of your business or idea before you spend the kind of money required to bring a private offering to investors. Truth be told, there are many types of business that don't lend themselves to this type of cost and effort because the likelihood of success in a private offering is slim.

For instance, a simple retail business is not a good candidate unless you have demonstrated success with the retail model and you have a plan to expand locations or franchise the idea.

A retail business based on pro forma financials alone from an entrepreneur who has never had experience in retail or owned a retail establishment wouldn't likely get much of a look or interest from me.

Many investors look for the unique twist to an existing business model or an idea that has a chance to be first to market. In other words, you have to be very, very good at differentiating yourself from every other business that has a similar market.

First, have an independent valuation performed on your business. This valuation will be based on a comprehensive business plan, audited financials, and a five-year set of projections (pro forma financials). A professional valuation firm can help you determine the value of your business.

If you have ever watched an episode of Shark Tank® on television, you will recognize this is the starting point at which each potential entrepreneur offers shares in his or her company for a percentage ownership. If you watch closely, when deals break down, valuation of the business is typically where it goes south. In most cases, the entrepreneur has an over-inflated idea of what his or her business is worth to an investor.

Following closely behind, the mistake most entrepreneurs make when seeking private investment, other than an unsubstantiated valuation, is demonstrating the *exact* details of how any funds raised will be used to move the business forward. If the majority of funds are designed to create a salary for the owner or owners, you've just wasted your time and money. A savvy investor wants his stake to be invested in someone who also has a vested interest with either his or her own money at stake or the investment of time and sweat equity.

When I see a business plan where the majority of the use of investment funds is to pay salaries, I promptly stop reading the offering. My co-founder and I at Teligistics went over two years before any salary was drawn by either of us.

If you are a student of Shark Tank® (and I encourage you to be one), hopefully you have realized that the value of a business to a potential investor is not how many hours of sweat equity you have invested, nor is it reflective of the money you yourself have invested, your sacrifices or your projections. It is the cold hard truth of revenue and profits, period. Of course, part of the equation is the existence of any intellectual property you may own (patents, etc.), market share, future marketability and growth potential.

But, at the end of the day, it is what you have booked to date in revenue and profit with the potential of more of both that makes the difference. It is also whether they believe in you and/or the management team's ability to execute the business plan.

There are firms that specialize in business valuations, and I warn you up front that they are expensive to get done correctly. But, if you are determined to raise capital in this method, it is important to get it right.

A private 504(D) offering limits the number of shareholders and requires a shareholders' agreement and a formal subscription document. These are legal documents that require professional legal advice. Do not attempt to construct a formal private offering on your own unless you like the prospect of shareholder lawsuits later.

It is valuable, however, to study how these arrangements work, as even a smaller equity ownership prospectus to individual investors should follow the same basic format with a business plan, existing and pro forma financials, and an investment document or agreement of some kind.

Because the private offering vehicle by itself is not a guarantee of success, it requires marketing. At Teligistics, we had a network of other business owners and angel investors that we had developed over the years of being in business in other ventures, etc. Get to know the angel investment clubs in your areas and attend the events. Most universities and some community colleges also have an angel investor network and host events.

New to the Gig Economy is the advent of crowd funding and

Kickstarter sites on the web. Today, even limited success with launching a private offering on those sites at lower funding amounts can sometimes evolve into larger investment opportunities, especially if you are able to deliver on your stated goals and objectives.

During the one-year period when our offering was available, my co-founder and I were on the road every night. This is literally the definition of the "road show" that is generally attributed to an initial public offering (IPO). When a company is set to launch an IPO, the underwriting securities firm that is bringing the company to the public stock market does a road show to present the business to stockbrokers, analysts and investors during the months preceding the public offering in an effort to build interest in the stock.

During this period, not only were we responsible for reaching the funding goal of the offering, but we still had to run Teligistics! In many cases, the funding of a business can be a serious distraction from actually running it. In our case, most of our evenings were spent with individual angel investor prospects after working more than a full day in the business.

Most formal private offerings are limited to sophisticated investors as described by the SEC and who sign off in the stock subscription document that they are, in fact, sophisticated investors who can afford to lose their entire investment.

When you entertain investments from family and friends who are not sophisticated investors, you need a document that explains they could lose their entire investment if the business fails. Handshake agreements seldom work and I don't recommend them.

There are several sources in which to explore writing your private offering and they can range from a law firm with a securities law practice (recommended) to an actual securities firm.

Whenever you take your business plan or idea to anyone, whether a potential investor, securities firm or anyone, for that matter, make sure you have them sign a non-disclosure agreement (NDA). This is especially true if you have any unique business strategies, intellectual properties or plan to be first to market with a product or service. Standard NDAs are available online, but I recommend you hire a competent business attorney for this document to be assured you are afforded certain protections from someone stealing your ideas.

Lessons Learned:

▶ *Consider angel investors if your business idea needs additional capital you cannot supply yourself.*

▶ *Debt and equity are the two main structures of an investment vehicle into a private enterprise and sometimes an investment deal involves both.*

▶ *Never give up controlling interest in the early stages of the business. Later, when the business is worth more, it may make sense to consider giving up controlling interest if the result is a greater net worth.*

▶ *Seek crowdfunding as an early start-up financing vehicle, but always consider the fact that you may need additional capital later, so do not give up too much equity early. You may need that equity for a later round of financing.*

▶ *Any investment into your business by an outsider requires some type of document to dictate the terms, payback, interest rate (if applicable), etc. Do not do this on a handshake, even if the investor is family. Protect yourself by getting any loan or investment in writing.*

▶ *Remember, taking money from family or friends has a special element of danger, drama and stress. Make sure your investors can afford to lose every dime they invest.*

▶ *When I have invested my own money with family members, I consider it gone when I give it to them. It's easier that way.*

▶ *A formal private offering under Section 504(D) requires you to hire a licensed securities firm or securities attorney. Do not attempt this by yourself.*

▶ *Be prepared to spend a significant amount of money on a business valuation by a reputable firm.*

▶ *Part of the offering document will be an in-depth business plan, pro forma financials, etc. You will need an accounting firm or CPA.*

▶ *It is not uncommon for a start-up or ongoing business concern to spend between $50k-$100K+ on the legal, accounting and valuation fees to produce a legitimate private offering.*

▶ *Getting the private offering document done is only the beginning. You will have to meet with potential angel and institutional investors to sell them on the idea of investing.*

▶ *Your chances of landing angel investors are exponentially better if you have proven you can execute the business plan and have existing revenue and profits.*

▶ *Business owners typically overvalue the worth of their business, which is why you need professional advice.*

▶ *A clear "use of funds" strategy is critical to an investor and should not be used to fund the entrepreneur's salary.*

CHAPTER 18

RULE #1 & #2 IN BUSINESS...
THE TEN MOST COMMON BUSINESS
MISTAKES THAT RESULT IN FAILURE

"Financial freedom is our birthright, rather than the 'slave walk' of the Monday through Friday grind."

—Suze Orman
American Author, Entrepreneur & TV Host

My two most important rules for being in business deal with issues that sink businesses every day. These issues are very preventable, but it takes practiced discipline to recognize and react to them.

At the top of the heap when it comes to business blunders, these two mistakes can be fatal to a business almost immediately.

Rule #1 in business: You can't spend more than you make. You may be able to do it short term while you have available capital, for instance, but a burn rate is not something to be proud of. If it's necessary to have a burn rate with sustained losses, you better have enough capital and moxie to get through it. The laws of financial management are just as sure as the law of physics.

There are a lot of examples. For instance, Amazon continually shows losses (except for fiscal year 2013 as of this writing), but its business model continues to attract capital because of the bet by investors that Amazon will deliver on its model and drive share-holder value. Even Amazon at some point will have to cross over into permanent profitability.

Every move within a business has to be scripted with the impact to the financial health as the underlying template.

It's one thing to have negative cash flow for a period if it is planned and if you have the proper resources, measures and contingencies in place.

Unbelievably, many business owners have no idea they are upside down, losing money every day and every month, until all of a sudden they are out of cash or can't make payroll.

The disciplined entrepreneur has a scheduled monthly close of his or her books and a profit and loss statement to study. It is important to look for trends, and the number one trend I go to in a financial statement is cash. Is cash being depleted or is the cash balance rising? A business can, for instance, have cash balances decreasing but still be making money as more cash is tied up in a growing accounts receivable balance.

Just like your personal finances, you should know the exact cash position of your business, as well as accounts receivable and accounts payable aging.

Rule #2 in business: the very nanosecond you realize you made a bad hire, end it! Nothing is more disruptive and destructive to a company than a bad hire, with the possible exception of the divorce of the owners.

Too often in my business career I have made a bad hire. We all do. If you're the first person to make all great hires, I'll be really mad!

There are many different types of problems created by a bad hire, but the reason they are a bad hire can be something you completely missed in the hiring process or because the employee was simply clever and was able to disguise his or her true self.

Without being a psychologist, I can boil down employee problems to a list of these typical traits:

1. Inability to get along with others
2. Attitude problems
3. Personality disorders (pick one of many)
4. No work ethic/lazy
5. Culture clash
6. Troublemaker by nature
7. Lack of character
8. Hypochondriac
9. Greedy

Now that is a fairly broad list. I've had entire departments in my companies turn dysfunctional only to find out that eliminating the bad apple usually cures it. Sometimes it is more than one bad apple. What's important is identifying it at the earliest stage possible, then terminating it.

I have tried to rehabilitate employees at considerable cost. Most small businesses neither have the time nor the resources to do this effectively. The sad fact is that many of these people need professional help.

One segment of business that seems to keep more dead weight and bad actors than any other is in sales. I have definitely had my share of sales people whom we have kept on payroll way too long.

The simple fact is that a small business cannot afford to pay underperforming or problem employees in sales or any other area. Imagine an employee with a bad attitude dealing with your customers. You may never know what it actually costs you in lost business until much later.

Our nature tries to rehabilitate problem employees, some of it driven by the ridiculous regulatory environment we find ourselves in regarding labor laws.

Employees in my ventures sign employment contracts that define their job descriptions and performance metrics. It's up to the employer to document metrics that are missed. This usually provides enough of a paper trail to justify termination, but check with your state laws. I'm fortunate to live in and have my businesses in a right-to-work state. If you are not in a right-to-work state, ridding yourself of a problem employee is much more difficult. Check with a labor attorney on your current labor laws.

In addition to an employment contract, my people sign non-compete and non-disclosure agreements. Any prospective employee not willing to sign these agreements does not get hired. In these agreements, we do not prevent an employee from getting a job in the same industry, but we don't allow them to have a competitive advantage simply by the knowledge they gained while working for us or by having contact with our clients.

We have been to court successfully several times to enforce these agreements. It's important, if this happens to you, that you follow through on it. Employees who have designs to leave your employ and steal trade secrets or customers will take notice and will hesitate or wisely reconsider.

Fortunately, most mistakes that kill a business are the preventable kind. Sometimes there are extraneous circumstances that are unpreventable, such as Hurricane Ike wiping a restaurant right off its slab! But, even in that scenario, a business owner who has cash and the proper insurance has the ability to recover.

Mistake #1 – Spending more than you take in (See Rule #1). Make sure you have a budget and stick to it.

Mistake #2: Hanging on to an employee too long that should have been immediately terminated (See Rule #2). Repeated instances of this mistake can destroy your business.

Mistake #3: Making it too hard for customers to give you their money. How many times have you been in a big box store and seen ten empty cash registers and twenty people in line at the only manned register? Whatever your product or service is, make sure it is extremely easy for customers to pay you for it by offering different methods.

Mistake #4: Pricing your products or services too low. Many times this mistake is simply made by not knowing what it actually costs to make your product or provide your service. If you don't know what your underlying costs are, how can you price it properly? Make sure ALL overhead costs are embedded in your pricing, not just the cost of goods.

I've done the low-price volume thing and the high-end, high-touch approach, and I can tell you that your customers buy based on perceived value. If your services or products are highly valued, customers will pay more. If all of your competition is lower than you, you better be able to demonstrate the added value of a higher price. If you are in a highly commoditized industry with slim margins (less than 40 percent), you have to find a way to add value that differentiates you from your competition in order to charge more.

Mistake #5: No timely financials. I insist on a hard close of my businesses monthly. This means we pick a date, close out the books for the month, produce a profit and loss statement, pay any taxes due, and make any necessary adjustments to improve the outlook for the next month.

Most businesses whose management does not have the discipline for this monthly process are likely committing mistake #1 (spending more than they make).

Every day I see my cash balances, and my accounts receivable and accounts payable aging for all my businesses. It is part of the financial literacy that begins at the personal level.

Managing accounts receivable is a critically important function. A cash business won't typically have accounts receivable other than possibly credit card transactions. However, if you have accounts receivable and your average collection timeframe takes longer than the period most of your business expenses are due, you have a negative cash flow problem that can sink your business.

Accounts receivable financing at a bank may help bridge the gap. Factoring (selling accounts receivable) should be a last resort as the fees are high and there is still some stigma to this type of financing, which will be seen on the invoices you send to customers.

You must stay on top of your receivables at all times. Accounts that are overdue should be called religiously. Accounts that cannot pay on time are usually the ones you make the least amount of money on. Sometimes a purge of late-paying customers is a good thing!

Mistake #6: Not paying your taxes and/or not paying them on time. We made a bad decision worse in my first airfreight venture by delaying the payment of taxes, hoping that cash flow and business would improve. Six quarters later, we owed the IRS six figures plus interest and penalties.

Cut everywhere else if you have to. Taxes do not go away. They will dog you forever until they are paid, even to the extent that the IRS will levy you personally. The IRS is especially sensitive to the withholding taxes you deduct from employees. They consider it literally stealing if these are not paid on time and will show up at your place of business, confiscate your bank accounts and make your life a living hell.

Mistake #7: Not relying on professionals. There are obviously things in your business you are good at. For the important things you aren't good at, hire the best professionals you can afford. This is especially true when it comes to accounting, taxes, payroll and legal advice.

Mistake #8: No clear marketing strategy or budget for it. Many entrepreneurs believe (at least in the beginning) that by building a better mousetrap, customers will line up to buy it. They won't if they don't know about it.

Who are your ideal customers and how do you find them? How will you drive sales and customers to your product, store or website? Are you good at social marketing?

Don't be the best-kept secret nobody has ever heard of. Part of your budget must include a marketing plan for strategic advertising and promotion.

Mistake #9: Overly optimistic revenue expectations. I am amazed at the business plans I see where there are lofty revenue projections, yet little detail on their marketing strategy or for how they obtain customers.

There is not one single pro forma financial that we have hit exactly on the numbers, even with the help of expert professionals. It's sometimes more of an art than a science, but you have to be realistic. You need a best and worst case scenario for planning budgets, expansion and product development.

Do not base your purchases, inventory and expenses on a best-case scenario.

Mistake #10: Failure to adapt to changes. Recently I went back and reviewed the original business plan we put together for Teligistics over eighteen years ago. Today, Teligistics' business model doesn't even remotely resemble the original business plan.

At Teligistics, we have adapted with the changing technologies and needs of our customers as they have evolved. What worked for us in 2001 doesn't necessarily work for us today.

Chief among the drivers of change is technology. An entrepreneur's willingness to recognize change and adapt accordingly can spell the difference between a short-term business idea and long-term success.

Social marketing is a great example. Many businesses have failed to learn, adapt and apply the benefits of social marketing to their own detriment.

It is definitely all right to be completely sold out to your business model — and you should be. But don't be so rigid that you can't recognize trends and changes in the market that can benefit your business by adapting as necessary.

Lessons Learned:

▶ *Study the ten most common mistakes made by businesses and entrepreneurs.*

▶ *Make a list, and put it somewhere you see it daily to remind yourself to take the necessary steps to avoid these mistakes.*

▶ *These ten items should be on a checklist you look at as you review your monthly financials.*

▶ *All ten of these mistakes can be fatal for your business by themselves; however, combining two or more will increase the odds of failure.*

▶ *Most of these mistakes are self-inflicted.*

CHAPTER 19

SO YOU WANT A PARTNER?

"It is rare to find a partner who is selfless. If you are lucky it happens once in a lifetime."

—*Michael Eisner*
Former CEO of Disney, Businessman & Author

If, as many government statistics bear out, greater than 50 percent of marriages end in divorce, the failure rate of business partnerships is likely much higher.

Make no mistake; entering into a business partnership is much like a marriage, whether it is just one other person or a business with many partners. Picking a partner in business, like a life partner, has serious consequences. I've been involved with a very successful partnership and have had several that were not so good, including one with a family member that was disastrous.

Partnerships can fail for many reasons, but have additional potential fatal mistakes not listed in the previous list of the Ten Fatal Business Mistakes.

There are many considerations you must confront when taking on a business partner. First, do your personalities click with each other? Seriously, if listening to your potential business partner talk or discuss business is akin to fingernails on a chalk board, the partnership is doomed no matter what the partner brings to the table.

Probably the most critical aspect to considering a partnership is, do you genuinely like the person? If you do, that helps. However, let's say your potential business partner has a specialized skill, such as code writing or programming, but you have the marketing genius. There are partnerships wherein the diversity of skills each brings to the table can offset some of the personality differences, but it's a tricky proposition.

Once you have decided a partnership is the route you want to take for your business, it is critical that you have a controlling document for your partnership business, almost like a governing constitution, commonly known as a partnership agreement. Think of it as a "pre-nup" for your business.

Here is a list of the topics you should cover in your mutual partnership agreement:

1. What percentage of the business do you each own? (See more on this below)

2. A detailed description of what each partner is responsible for (job duties, etc.). Think of this in terms of a detailed job description.

3. An agreement on how salaries are paid, how much to whom, and when the business will be able to pay any salaries. Think of this as an employment agreement for each of the partners.

4. A buy/sell provision detailing an agreed-to formula if one partner wants out. This is also important for a liquidity event (sale of business or an infusion of institutional capital). Make sure the agreement states

what happens in the case of the death of one of the partners (most don't want to be in business with the partner's wife or family by default). If necessary, fund a key man life insurance policy to fund the buyout upon a death. If the partners are in good health, term life insurance is a good vehicle for this. A buy/sell agreement is only as good as your ability to fund it. The buy/sell agreement must include an agreed-to methodology for the valuation of the worth of the company, and therefore the value of the equity of the deceased partner or partner who is departing for whatever reason.

5. If any partner provided loans or funding to the business that needs to be paid back, it is vital that a loan document or other agreed-to documentation is reflected in the partnership agreement.

The partnership agreement needs to be reviewed and modified on a regular or as-needed basis. In my business organizations, the business models changed over time, as did the needs, funding and structures of the businesses. Consider the partnership document a living and breathing document. It must be updated annually.

I have seen otherwise successful businesses and owners literally come apart at the seams because this process is not followed.

The reason for partnership failures can be numerous but, other than the Ten Fatal Business Mistakes in Chapter 18, unique to these businesses are some very common themes:

1. Simple greed. One partner feels like he or she deserves more of the rewards, income or equity.

2. Fairness. One partner is perceived to work more hours or dedicates more time and effort to the business.

3. Spouses. A spouse will have much influence over the partner. Make sure you don't enter a partnership with someone whose spouse you can't stand.

4. Divorce. Nothing (other than the death of a key partner) can be as disruptive as a business partner becoming involved in a hotly contested divorce of one of the partners.

5. Overvaluation of partners' worth. Sometimes partners have an overly optimistic opinion of the value they bring to the partnership and create unreasonable expectations, leading to #1 above.

6. Hiring family in the business (nepotism). Want to really complicate a partnership... bring in family members!

7. Partner tires of or loses interest in the business.

8. Conflicts of interest. Make sure your agreement covers outside business interests.

9. Death of a partner.

When a business partnership works, it's a beautiful thing. From what I have experienced, successful business partnerships are those whose partners are unselfish and where each partner brings a special talent or expertise to the table that the other partners(s) may not have. It could also be that each partner enjoys the niche or responsibilities he or she performs. For instance, one partner may hate sales while another loves it.

When looking at potential partners, you must analyze what the partner brings to the table that would increase the value of the business.

Make sure you can distinguish the difference between an investor and a partner. On numerous occasions, I have had potential investors want to be active partners. The truth of the matter was that the only thing I needed from those investors was their investment and possibly their contacts, but I did not want them to be involved in running the day-to-day operations and decisions of the business.

Although not one to judge, I would scrutinize a potential partner's previous business situations very closely before establishing a partnership. If a potential partner has had numerous contentious business relationships, or even litigation with other business partners, I would think long and hard about accepting that person as a partner. I would scrutinize their previous business situation very closely.

The same goes with potential partners who are on their third, fourth or fifth marriages. If they have proven that they can't keep a relationship together, and continually repeat the process, *they* are probably the common denominator and there would have to be a compelling reason to consider them as potential partners. Under those types of conditions, their unique value would have to be extraordinary and the partnership agreement would need to be ironclad.

Lessons Learned:

► *When you have the right partner, a business partner-ship can leverage the partners' individual skillsets and move the business forward faster.*

► *Partnerships spread the risk and the workload. Also, it's helpful to have someone with the same vested inter-*

est to challenge and discuss the business model on an ongoing basis.

▶ *Partnerships have unique challenges that can add an extra layer of complexity to a business.*

▶ *A business partnership SHOULD plan for a partner divorce as if it is inevitable and have a written buy/sell agreement in place for any contingency, including a partner death, disability and disputes.*

▶ *Business partnerships need written partnership agreements, spelling out the duties, responsibilities and detailed job definition of each partner.*

▶ *Both the partnership agreements and buy/sell should be updated annually, as business models change over time, as do the partners' interest and participation levels.*

▶ *Avoid potential partners who have demonstrated the inability to sustain long-term business and personal relationships.*

▶ *An investor is not necessarily a good business partner when it comes to day-to-day operations of the business. Learn how to distinguish between the two.*

CHAPTER 20

THE FAMILY BUSINESS

"Competing agendas make for harsh office politics. Fights happen in the family, too, but when the goal is to help the family business win, turf battles diminish. We're much faster than companies that have to go through a more politicized process of getting things done."

—*Joel Schechter, CEO of Honora*
64 Year-Old Family Global Jewelry Business

Few things in life can match the sheer joy of a well-run, successful family-owned business.

The family-owned small business is the backbone of the American success story. The immigrants who came to America typically had the entire family vested in the operation of their small business, no matter what it was.

There are many rewards and unique challenges for family-owned businesses.

Many businesses started out with a sole proprietor and, as the business grew, spouses and family members pitched in and ultimately became valuable and permanent fixtures in the business.

As with partnerships, family-owned businesses typically are a reflection of the successful relationships within the family — or of the dysfunction that might exist. A family-owned business will expose and illuminate the current state of the family relationships.

Trust amongst family members in the business is one of the strongest assets of this type of business.

My wife and I learned very early in our relationship that we get along much better if we don't work together. Some marriages can thrive in this environment but, for some reason, we seem to function better as life partners when we don't work in the same business together. The fortunate thing for us is we both recognized this as a couple, together. In fact, it's been somewhat of a running joke between us for years.

I can't imagine how difficult it would be to be in a family business with a spouse when there are problems in the spousal relationship. I can guarantee you the business would suffer, as both employees and customers pick up on this negative vibe all too quickly.

Many businesses that start off as part-time micro businesses start to fill positions with family members as the business grows. One advantage with family-owned businesses is that everyone generally pulls in the same direction for the benefit of the family.

However, it is important to note that the same jealousies, pettiness and laziness can infect a family employee just as it can a regular employee in any business. What is common is that there is generally a patriarch or matriarch who is the principal driver or entrepreneur that the entire family looks to for leadership.

A family-owned business takes the shape of family relationships in the business whether they are great or dysfunctional. A dysfunctional family-owned business will typically implode at a much faster rate than a dysfunctional non-family owned businesses. In a business that is not family-owned, the owners don't necessarily return to the same home after work hours. In a family-owned business, whatever issues family members had at the office are usually brought home with them, so they never get a "cooling off" period.

When you're running a family-owned business, it's easy to let your guard down when it comes to family staff member responsibilities. Whereas many family members take pride in the quality of the product or service put forward to customers, some will try to skate by; after all, sometimes a family member may think he or she has "tenure" by the sheer fact of his or her last name or bloodline and think they can't be fired.

Most highly successful family-owned businesses have fully delineated responsibilities, duties and controls, just as if no family members were employed.

Successful businesses of this type have key family staff members who can be fully counted on. The camaraderie in a family-owned business is palpable.

Because many family-owned businesses have a quintessential patriarch or matriarch, many don't survive a second generation, or the business might decline on a generational basis unless very strong leadership and well-developed processes are engrained in the business.

Think about it. The original entrepreneur had the original vision, sacrifices and drive. Many times the business overcame obstacles just on the sheer force of that person's will or their flat persistence.

Will a second generation who walks into a ready-made position have this same drive? It's possible, but only if the pride of the family name and the recognition of their predecessor's sacrifices are fully understood and appreciated.

It takes a unique individual and some of the same traits as the founder(s) to take the original family entrepreneur's dream and not only carry it forward but grow it for future generations.

The family-owned business entrepreneur will sometimes skip the formalities that most businesses use with their employees, such as written job descriptions, accountability and other normal business structures. That modus operandi needs to change the minute a non-family member is brought into the fold as an employee.

I have family members spread throughout my organizations, which provides some strategic advantages. First, I get the true low-down on ground-level operations, customer interactions and general in-house politics that I might not get with a non-family employee.

The downsides of having a family member involved in the business should be obvious but, if not, here's a few:

1. If the family member is NOT doing MORE than the average employee, he or she will build a general resentment from most, if not all, of the non-family staff. They will believe that person, had he or she not been family, would have never gotten the job.

2. Be ready to back up a promotion for a family member when he or she is promoted over someone with more tenure. Promoting a family member over a good employee "just because" will breed roots of resentment that will fester into a company-wide cancer.

3. Make sure family members know, beyond a shadow of a doubt, that your expectation is that they do MORE for the business than just somebody that is there for a paycheck.

4. Do NOT discuss family issues in front of staff. Nothing is more embarrassing or de-edifying than a family member calling out the boss because he or she takes too long in the bathroom at home!

5. Treat family members as well as you would any other employee, but let them know, beyond a shadow of a doubt, that you have higher expectations for them.

6. Family-owned businesses are oftentimes guilty of Rule #2 in business: hanging onto a family member as staff when they are the root of all disruption, are insubordinate, or are a general pain. It is more difficult to fire a family member than a regular staffer because of the family implications but, in most instances, you need to make this change faster than normal.

The successful family-owned businesses have learned how to create an environment of teamwork and trust that can be stronger than traditional non-family businesses.

Lessons Learned:

▶ *Understand the unique challenges of a family-owned business and plan to deal with those specific challenges head on with processes and procedures.*

▶ *Many second-generation businesses don't succeed because they never learned the entrepreneurial skills from the founder that made the business work in the first place — or the proper processes and controls were never put into place for the business survivorship.*

▶ *Don't bring family issues into the business, and especially don't discuss them among other employees.*

▶ *Successful family-owned businesses have the same controls and processes in place, just as any normal business.*

▶ *Trust and camaraderie are two valuable tangible assets that make family-owned businesses different.*

▶ *Family members must be able to "turn off" the switch when together so that not every waking moment together is a business meeting. (This is very hard to do during a start-up phase over sheer excitement, and that's okay!)*

▶ *Running a family-owned business means every major business decision has an extra degree of importance as you take into consideration how it affects a family member.*

▶ *A family member who is a bad employee is worse than an employee nobody is related to. Bad apples that are from the same tree have a propensity to infect the rest of the staff at an alarming rate. Recognize this in its earliest stages and make the tough decision to boot a non-performing family member. You might have family relationships to repair, but make sure family members understand that they are held to a higher standard.*

CHAPTER 21

RENEGADE MARKETING®

"Focus on the core problem your business solves and put out lots of content, enthusiasm and ideas about how to solve that problem."

—Laura Fitton
Founder of Oneforty.com, Co-Author of Twitter for Dummies

D o not confuse *Renegade Marketing®* with advertising. Even though advertising might be a portion of your overall marketing strategy, many business owners make the mistake of advertising via a "mud on the wall" approach.

I've owned businesses that had very different approaches to win customers. In the airfreight business, we relied on personal relationship selling and customer entertainment to win and keep clients. In the days before the Internet, it wasn't unusual for us to be making donut runs in the morning, lunches during the day and beer runs on Friday afternoons to the shipping docks of our best customers and those we were targeting to steal from our competition.

Today, that approach still works to some degree; however, the decisions for large account logistics are usually made at a much higher level than the shipping manager and require a professional sales and marketing approach to win large enterprise-level deals.

We never spent one penny on advertising, other than an occasional little league team sponsorship. Our marketing dollars were spent on personal client relationships and directly on our customers. Even if I had put ten billboards on every freeway in Houston, it wouldn't have made one shipping manager call us, even though it would have increased our brand awareness.

The problem with most small businesses is that they don't have the money to create a "brand awareness" campaign. All marketing needs to be extremely targeted to likely customers until a budget can be established for mass marketing and building your brand.

Until you can afford it, building your brand will have to come from very satisfied customers.

At Teligistics, we stair-stepped our marketing approach to a point where we have become the recognized subject matter experts regarding contracts and the sourcing of large enterprise-level global telecommunications deals, using *Renegade Marketing®* techniques.

In the beginning, about all we had was our expert knowledge about how large companies make huge financial and liability decisions when procuring telecom services. We crafted these into "white papers," providing case studies or just enough information on how we solve the critical issues of procuring telecom contracts without giving away our trade secrets. To get these white papers, you had to fill out a form (which came directly to me) on our website, then I would send the white papers out via email and follow up with a phone call — and thus the sales process was started.

How would we drive traffic to the website? We had a small budget for Google ads and chose our key words very carefully.

Also, in building the website, our designers took search engine optimization (SEO) into careful consideration. When a prospective client searched for key words, we would usually pop up in the first three listings on Google.

For us, we knew *exactly* what problems we could solve for our customers and we could quantify it and prove out the ROI. Do you know what problem your business or idea would solve?

Our business model was and still is a business-to-business (B2B) one. We don't sell products or services to consumers. But, make no mistake; even if your business sells cupcakes, it is solving some kind of problem — a sudden urge for chocolate or a sugary treat!

Even if your business is making hamburgers, what problem do you solve, and how are you better than your competitors? Remember earlier in the book when I mentioned you don't necessarily want your customers buying from you simply because you're perceived as cheaper.

In my experience, customers buy from businesses for the following reasons or combination of reasons:

1. They simply like you (or your salesperson).

2. Your product or service fulfills a need, whether it's life-sustaining (ex: insulin injection needles, or even food), convenience, pleasure, security, peace of mind, prestige or status.

3. Your product or service makes life easier.

4. Your product or service makes their job easier.

5. Your product or service has a proven ROI.

6. Your product or service creates a new need (ex: the latest smartphone).

7. Your product or service is cheaper (only if it is a commodity).

I could give you many examples of why people buy, but I'll use a Rolex® watch as an example. Most everyone needs to know what time it is, and the wristwatch has been around for a hundred years.

What makes a person spend $10,000 on a Rolex® when they could buy a $25 Timex® watch?

Does the Rolex® keep better time? Possibly... but do a few seconds' difference a month between the two watches justify the cost difference?

People buy the Rolex® because of the prestige and status that goes along with it. It's the same reason a lady buys a $3200 Prada® purse as opposed to a $15 purse from Wal-Mart. The need for this perceived prestige and the want to have one of the finer things in life is purely human.

Why would someone want *your* cupcakes as opposed to what's sitting out at the local grocery store bakery? Do they taste better? Are they made with natural ingredients? Do you deliver (for birthday parties, etc.)? Can you customize them?

If you don't establish your product or service as a premium product or service, you will get lumped into a commodity category and be continually battling for customers on price.

Even if I had a businesses that was in commodity markets, such as a gas station located on a corner with three other gas stations on the opposite corners, I would have to learn and apply *Renegade Marketing®*.

How would I do this?

First of all, my gas station would be cleaner than the others. My gas station would be landscaped and well-lit. I would have items in my convenience store the others wouldn't carry, maybe some fresh fruit and vegetables. How about a free donut and cup of coffee with a fill up? My clerks would be extremely courteous, be able to speak clear English, and be uniformed. The bathrooms would be spotless. How about a loyalty program with rewards? For every five fill ups a free car wash?

I'd have a pump aisle where you could get premium service, with an attendant filling up your tank and cleaning your windows. (Yes, I'm old enough to remember when this was common and I miss it!) For this premium service, I would get an extra 5-10 cents per gallon. This is just for starters. I would literally *toast* my competition on the other three corners and charge my customers more per gallon and they would gladly pay. Think of the busy professionals, elderly and ladies who love to have this premium service, all without getting out of their vehicles.

To be a true disciple of *Renegade Marketing*®, you have to embrace and love competition. Ignore your competition at your own peril. A Renegade Marketer® is always one step or more ahead of his or her competition.

During our airfreight days, we hung out at the docks of the airlines' freight complex after we dropped off our shipments that were being airfreighted to different parts of the world. We saw large crates, valves, pumps, pallets and boxes of freight being dropped off by delivery services from competing airfreight companies.

The docks were a busy place in the evenings, but it was pretty simple to spend some time and make notes of the company labels who were shipping these profitable shipments, then follow up on them with our own sales staff. No more fishing around for leads. These shipments were from companies who were actually shipping freight out of Houston. We could see who was doing it and we would be in their warehouse the next day making our pitch to replace the freight forwarder who shipped their cargo the day before. We didn't wait for a focus group; we didn't wait to see if advertising paid off. We went to the source.

Over the years of dealing with thousands of customers of all types, there is absolutely nothing that replaces a personal relationship with customers who believe you really care about their well-being.

You must also become a social media expert or find somebody who is. But I must warn you: Very seldom have I seen social networking as the sole source of customers or customer growth. It must be another tool in the arsenal. For businesses that sell to other businesses, I have found LinkedIn and Twitter more successful for us than Facebook, but you have to have a presence on all three. By the time this book is published, there may be even more as InstaGram and Snap Chat have also picked up momentum.

The more your business is focused on retail sales of any kind, the more important social networking is. If you are not an expert at this, ask a millennial to help. They would rather communicate via social networking than actually have a live conversation in most instances!

I won't delve into the intricacies of social media here, as there are plenty of books and websites where you can learn. Find companies who have been successful with social media and follow their pattern. When I say "successful," I mean they have turned new customers into revenue solely from social media.

In today's world of business, not using social media is not an option.

Be creative. Our software solutions at Teligistics produce on average a 42 percent reduction in a large company's telecom costs. For publicly-traded companies, telecommunications and IT, costs are relatively easy to find on quarterly financial statements. We simply call up the chief financial officer or other central decision-maker and say we have a check for X amount of hundreds of thousands — or millions — of dollars to present to them. Guess how easy it is to get an appointment? Of course, this isn't a real check, but we have a designed marketing check already made out to bring to the meeting for a stunning visual effect of our solutions.

Pay "bird dog" fees or referral commissions to those who successfully introduce you to the decision-makers that result in a sale.

For the first few years, I drove one of our delivery vans home and everywhere I could. It had our company name on it and I was damned proud of it. Why not wrap your car with your business on it, especially if you sell to consumers?

Renegade Marketing® experts never try to sell or market their product or service with the "features." Our software has a U.S. patent and is proprietary. Impressive? So what? Today's customer wants to know how we solve *his* or *her* problems! They couldn't care less about the features of our solutions, only how those solutions will make their jobs easier to focus on other IT initiatives.

Today, our typical customers are pulled in so many different directions at the same time that it is almost impossible to reach them. People today go from one meeting to the next. It's a wonder any work gets done. You must be creative in how you reach these folks. The old cold-calling approach and mass media advertising just don't work anymore.

Even email has gotten blasé. I have sent repeated emails to C-level customers who never read them. Today, many broadcast their cell phone numbers on their business cards and directories. I'm much more successful at reaching people via text messaging, which is a phenomenon I avoided for as long as I could, but you can't wait any longer. No longer do I find people offended that I am trying to reach them by sending a text. One word of caution, though. Don't make someone have to text you back and ask, "Who is this?" Identify yourself in your original text message.

Know who your customers really are. I am stunned by the fact that many business owners cannot succinctly state who their primary customers are. If they don't know, how can they target their marketing or sales efforts?

In my publishing business, we published two of my political fiction action thrillers, *"Patriots of Treason"* in 2012, and the sequel, *"A State of Treason,"* in 2014. Both books have reached several bestseller lists.

You can bet we knew exactly who would read these books and focused our marketing efforts on websites and other areas where our potential readers visited. The results were phenomenal. We knew where our readers hung out online and we targeted those readers on blogs, review sites and media sites such as *The Drudge Report.*

As we have taken on more authors, we help them target the audiences that are candidates to buy and read their books.

Renegade Marketers® will termite their way through an account. What does this mean? Too many times we have seen complete regime changes in the IT departments of large companies. The CIO leaves, a new one comes in, and brings in his or her own people. What may have taken months or years to establish in long-term relationships is gone in a flash.

Termiting your way through a customer means that you make sure you have relationships at every level throughout the account. This means everyone from the lowest level contact you have all the way to the C-suite. I can promise you our clients know who Teligistics is in the C-suite, despite who we deal with on a daily basis.

If I was in the retail business, I would make it my mission to know our customers, how many kids they have, what their favorite products or menu items are, and when they celebrate their birthdays.

When's the last time a restaurant owner came to your table and asked how the food and service was? It happens all the time to me. You know why? Because I go out of my way to frequent establishments that genuinely care about where I spend my money.

You can't get this level of personal touch or relationships that build brand loyalty strictly from social media.

In fact, with the advent of the instantaneous tools that are available to the average consumer, a business better be paying close attention. When looking for a restaurant recently, my daughter was strictly relying on online reviews she pulled right up on her smartphone. She saw *one* bad review and the restaurant was eliminated as a possible choice.

One bad review???

Remember the old saying, "the customer is always right"?

Well, they may not actually be right, but what's important is their perception. Their perception is their own reality. I can't tell you how many times I've swallowed my pride to keep a customer happy — to a point. But the effort needs to be made. I've read in the past that a bad customer experience spoken by mouth will reach 254 people on average. With social media and online reviews, you can figure this reputation hit will be exponential.

In your early stages, or even when you are trying to pick up new customers in an existing business, try providing samples or trial projects to get your foot in the door. Giving a potential customer who happens to stop in a fresh chocolate cupcake is a lot cheaper than buying advertising. The key is *conversion*. Convert that trial or freebie into a long-term repeat customer.

I've seen some marketing campaigns that were well orchestrated, but lacked in follow up. Why would an organization spend the money to get its message out to people, only to fail to follow through with the next steps to convert them to customers? It would be easier just to flush that money down the toilet.

Educate your potential customers. People are hungry for information; they don't want to be sold to. The old manipulative closing techniques are outdated. Typical consumers today, whether retail consumers or B2B consumers, are much more well-informed today and can instantly do the research they need to make a buying decision, with or without you.

Make sure YOU are the expert they come to, whether it's controlling the economics of IT or the best damn chocolate cupcake in the world!

Lessons Learned:

▶ *For ANY kind of marketing, it's critical that you know exactly WHO your business's customers are.*

▶ *Nothing in the world takes the place of personal relationships. Get to know your customers. Customers who feel appreciated keep coming back to spend money!*

▶ *The best brand advertising you can do is to have a great product or service with outstanding customer service.*

▶ *Startups and young businesses can burn through a lot of money building a brand without any customers. Any money budgeted for marketing must bring in customers when your budget is tight.*

▶ *No advertising campaign can be deemed successful until you know its conversion rate which, despite what you may read anywhere else, is paying customers derived from that advertising.*

▶ *Social media is a necessary component of Renegade Marketing®. You must become a semi-expert in social media (or hire one) or risk losing a large and growing segment of potential customers. This is also the least expensive method for building a brand.*

▶ *Learn how to termite your way through accounts if your business is B2B. Have relationships at every level, which gives you the best chance to survive regime changes, key personnel leaving the company, etc.*

▶ *Renegade Marketing® is utilizing aggressive non-typical marketing approaches. If all your competition is doing things one way, consider doing the opposite. Be bold. Stand out. Succeed!*

▶ *Understand that the majority of your marketing efforts will fail. Like a ship traveling the ocean, you must continually adjust your navigational compass to stay on track through marketing failures (storms) or efforts that don't produce the desired results. Stay the course!*

▶ *Embrace competition, but beat their pants off!*

CHAPTER 22

THE TAX MAN COMETH & THE FUTURE OF FREE ENTERPRISE

"Just what do we tax under our current system? Work, that's what. Hard work and productivity. The harder you work, the more you achieve. The more you achieve, the more you're taxed. To make matters worse, under our "progressive" income tax system, the harder you work, the more severe the punishment actually is!"

—*Neal Boortz*
FairTax.org Advocate, Radio Host, Author & Attorney

E arlier in this book, I stated that this may be the best time in history to start a business, and it is!

You won't start or run a business and become *unemployable* in a vacuum. Policies set forth by our elected leaders, whether they be local, state or federal, have consequences.

However, I would be remiss if I also didn't note that there are serious threats to free enterprise in America. Among those threats, in no particular order, are:

1. Unsustainable debt

2. The progressive income tax

3. The rise of socialism in America

4. Lack of term limits for elected officials

All of us must keep our personal and business finances in check, balancing our checkbooks and paying down debt. Why shouldn't we demand this from our elected leaders for our government's finances? My personal opinion (and that of many economic experts) is that there will be a reckoning at some point, possibly crashing the value of the U.S. dollar. That would be catastrophic, and no business or citizen would escape the dire consequences that would bring.

We need to demand of our political leaders a balanced budget constitutional amendment!

It's no secret that the cost associated with complying with a 72,000-page tax code is outrageous. How did America reach the point where it is acceptable to tax productivity? Taxing income is taxing work and is anti-American!

Recent revelations of IRS targeting of political enemies makes it even more urgent to end the current tax code and deep-six the IRS. Economic study after study proves that a national consumption-based tax is the answer to ridding ourselves of this KGB-style agency, the ridiculous tax code and taxes on income forever!

And don't believe the flat tax crowd, as politicians will NEVER keep a tax flat. They have proven that over the last hundred years.

As a new member of the *unemployable* family, you will get to see the burden put on small business (and large business) with the regulatory issues surrounding the income tax. You can no longer sit on the sideline and be silent. It's inherent on you to participate in the political system and help rid our country of this pariah.

America is less competitive in the world markets because of this personal and corporate income tax.

Get involved and be part of the solution. Support the fair tax and let your politicians know that you do!

The liberal policies of the last fifty years are catching up to us. Socialism is alive and growing at the same rate as the welfare state. Entitlements are now a lifestyle instead of a short-lived bridge to help someone over a temporary financial hump.

We can look all over the world at examples of the massive failure of socialism, with the latest example being Greece.

Since you are *unemployable*, the entitlement elite will keep looking to YOUR productivity to finance the endless regulatory burdens and wealth redistribution being touted by socialists.

Renegade Capitalists® are rugged individualists. We want government to get out of the way and limit the regulations, red tape and onerous taxes that curtail productivity.

I love the quote by former UK Prime Minister Margaret Thatcher who said, "Socialism works great until you run out of other people's money!"

Socialism is a serious threat to our freedom and to our goal of achieving and maintaining an *unemployable* lifestyle.

If you read enough of the early writings of our Founders, it will be apparent that they did not consider the possibility that anyone would want to make a career out of an elected office. In fact, America was founded on a citizen government where, if willing, you might run for office to do your part.

Today, elected officials have election campaign funds that act as slush funds whether they are elected or not. A defeated candidate who may have millions of dollars in his campaign instantly becomes a lobbyist.

Can you imagine someone in the private sector telling his or her employer, "I want to keep my job (but not do most of the associated duties in the job description) and continue to get paid while I campaign for a better, high-paying job?"

That wouldn't fly for two seconds...

EPILOGUE

I'm always amazed and humbled that I can put my thoughts on paper and someone would actually be entertained or find ideas in those writings useful, even enough to pay for it. My sincere thanks to you for allowing me to be a very small part of your busy lives.

Entrepreneurship, as you have probably gathered by now, is a passion for me. I love helping budding *Renegade Capitalists*® achieve their dreams.

If you would like further information on how we can help you move your business forward by assisting with a business plan evaluation, or if you are seeking angel investors, please visit us at www.renegadecapitalist.com.

"Charge for something and make more than you spend."

—*Marco Arment*
Founder of InstaPaper

Glossary for Unemployable!

Accounts Payable Aging—Process of determining which suppliers are being paid on time, which are not, and how far their bills are behind the payment date. This analysis indicates which supplier(s) must be paid first in order to avoid any credit or supply problem. *www.businessdictionary.com*

Accounts Receivable Financing—Using amounts owed by customers as collateral in raising a secured short-term loan on a one-time or on a continuous basis. In case of a default, the lender has the right to collect receivables directly from the named debtors of the firm. It is a type of 'off balance sheet' financing. Also called pledging of accounts receivable. See also discounting and factoring. *www.businessdictionary.com*

Amortization [Amortized Mortgage Amortization]—1. The gradual elimination of a liability, such as a mortgage, in regular payments over a specified period of time. Such payments must be sufficient to cover both principal and interest. *www.investorwords.com*

Analysis Paralysis—Analysis paralysis or paralysis by analysis is an anti-pattern, the state of over-analyzing (or over-thinking) a situation so that a decision or action is never taken, in effect paralyzing the outcome. *en.wikipedia.org*

Angel Investor—An angel investor or angel (also known as a business angel or informal investor or angel funder or private investor or seed investor) is an affluent individual who provides capital for a business start-up, usually in exchange for convertible debt or ownership equity. *en.wikipedia.org*

Assets—Something that an entity has acquired or purchased, and that has money value (its cost, book value, market value, or residual value). An asset can be (1) something physical, such as cash, machinery, inventory, land and building, (2) an enforceable claim against others, such as accounts receivable, (3) right, such as copyright, patent, trademark, or (4) an assumption, such as goodwill. *www.businessdictionary.com*

Balanced Budget Constitutional Amendment—The balanced budget amendment would prohibit the federal government from spending more than it takes in each year, unless Congress specifically authorizes the additional spending through a three-fifths or two-thirds vote. It would require the President to submit a balanced budget each year. And it would allow Congress to waive the balanced budget requirement when there is a declaration of war. *uspolitics.about.com*

Base Salary Limitations—"The financially literate sales entrepreneur will not be enslaved by base salary limitations. Those who are financially illiterate will be limited in their choice of sales positions, forced to take a job with limited potential but just enough base salary to cover their bills." *David Thomas Roberts, author of Unemployable!*

Base salary is a fixed amount of money paid to an employee by an employer in return for work performed. Base salary does not include benefits, bonuses or any other potential compensation from an employer. www.businessdictionary.com

Binary Plans (in Network Marketing)—Binary compensation plans are characterized by having two legs, and only two legs. This makes them very simple. Most binary comp plans will pay you commissions on your weak leg only – the smaller leg that has less volume. This keeps most people focused on building their weak leg, which is also known as the pay leg in a binary compensation plan. *successfulmlmtips.com*

Bootstrapping—"Low start-up investment. Bootstrapping is an efficient way to do a start-up business when capital is lacking." *David Thomas Roberts, author of Unemployable!*

Brand Awareness Campaign—Extent to which a brand is recognized by potential customers, and is correctly associated with a particular product. Expressed usually as a percentage of target market, brand awareness is the primary goal of advertising in the early months or years of a product's introduction. *www.businessdictionary.com*

Brand Loyalty—The extent of the faithfulness of consumers to a particular brand, expressed through their repeat purchases, irrespective of the marketing pressure generated by the competing brands. *www.businessdictionary.com*

Burn Rate—For a company with negative cash flow, the rate of that negative cash flow, usually per month. Often used by venture capitalists to measure how much time a startup has to reach positive cash flow before they run out of money or require additional funding. *www.investorwords.com*

Business Model—Description of means and methods a firm employs to earn the revenue projected in its plans. It views the business as a system and answers the question, "How are we going to make money to survive and grow?" *www.businessdictionary.com*

Business Plan—Set of documents prepared by a firm's management to summarize its operational and financial objectives for the near future (usually one to three years) and to show how they will be achieved. It serves as a blueprint to guide the firm's policies and strategies, and is continually modified as conditions change and new opportunities and/or threats emerge. When prepared for external audience (lenders, prospective investors) it details the past, present, and forecasted performance of the firm. And usually also contains pro-forma balance sheet, income statement, and cash flow statement, to illustrate how the financing being sought will affect the firm's financial position. *www.businessdictionary.com*

Business Processes—A series of logically related activities or tasks (such as planning, production, or sales) performed together to produce a defined set of results. *www.businessdictionary.com*

Business-to-Business (B2B)—Trading between firms (and not between businesses and consumers), characterized by (1) relatively large volumes, (2) competitive and stable prices, (3) fast delivery times and, often, (4) on deferred payment basis. In general, wholesaling is B2B and retailing is B2C. *www.businessdictionary.com*

Buy/Sell Provision—An agreement that states if a part-owner of a business wishes to sell, he or she must sell to the other part-owners or another person named in the agreement. The price of the part of the business is also named in the agreement. *www.businessdictionary.com*

Capital-Intensive—Industry requiring large sums of investment in purchase, maintenance, and amortization of capital equipment, such as automotive, petroleum, and steel industry. Capital intensive industries need a high volume of production and a high margin of profit (as well as low interest rates) to be able to provide adequate returns on investment. See also labor intensive. *www.businessdictionary.com*

Capitalism—A system of economics based on the private ownership of capital and production inputs, and on the production of goods and services for profit. The production of goods and services is based on supply and demand in the general market (market economy), rather than through central planning (planned economy). Capitalism is generally characterized by competition between producers. Other facets, such as the participation of government in production and regulation, vary across models of capitalism. *www.investopedia.com*

Cash Flow—Incomings and outgoings of cash, representing the operating activities of an organization. *www.businessdictionary.com*

Chronic Negativity—Being in a constant state of negativity.

C-Level Customers (also known as C-Suite Customers)—A widely-used slang term used to collectively refer to a corporation's most important senior executives. C-Suite gets its name because top senior executives' titles tend to start with the letter C, for chief, as in chief executive officer, chief operating officer and chief information officer. *www.investopedia.com*

Comfort Zone—The comfort zone is a psychological state in which a person feels familiar, at ease, in control and experiences low anxiety and stress. In the zone a steady level of performance is possible. *en.wikipedia.org*

Commodity Category—A reasonably interchangeable good or material, bought and sold freely as an article of commerce. Commodities include agricultural products, fuels, and metals and are traded in bulk on a commodity exchange or spot market. *www.businessdictionary.com*

Compensation Plan—In network marketing, the details of how the commission of independent agents will be determined on their own and their downline's sales revenue. See also compensation structure. *www.businessdictionary.com*

Competition—Economics: Rivalry in which every seller tries to get what other sellers are seeking at the same time: sales, profit, and market share by offering the best practicable combination of price, quality, and service. Where the market information flows freely, competition plays a regulatory function in balancing demand and supply. *www.businessdictionary.com*

Compounding Interest—Interest computed on the principal amount to which interest earned to-date has been added. Where compound interest is applied, the investment grows exponentially and not linearly as in the case of simple interest. Formula: Principal x {(Annual interest rate ÷ 100) + 1}^number of years. For example, $1,000 at an annual compound interest rate of 10 percent will, in 5 years, be: 1000 x {(10 ÷ 100) + 1}^5 = $1,6105.51. *www.businessdictionary.com*

Conflict of Interest—1. A situation that has the potential to undermine the impartiality of a person because of the possibility of a clash between the person's self-interest and professional interest or public interest. 2. A situation in which a party's responsibility to a second-party limits its ability to discharge its responsibility to a third-party. *www.businessdictionary.com*

Controlling Interest—Ownership of 51 percent or more of the voting-stock (shares) that gives the owner(s) legal control of a firm. *www.businessdictionary.com*

Conversion Rate—1. Commerce: Rate at which a commodity, currency, or a type of security can be exchanged for another. 2. Internet: Alternative term for hit rate. *www.businessdictionary.com*

"Cooling Off" Period—"In a family owned business, whatever issues family members had at the office are usually brought home with them, so they never get a 'cooling off' period." *David Thomas Roberts, author of Unemployable!*

Crab Theory—Crab mentality, sometimes referred to as crabs in the bucket, is a phrase that describes a way of thinking best described by the phrase "if I can't have it, neither can you." *en.wikipedia.org*

Credit Score—A measure of credit risk calculated from a credit report using a standardized formula. Factors that can damage a credit score include late payments, absence of credit references, and unfavorable credit card use. *www.investorwords.com*

Crowdfunding—Method of raising small amounts of money from a large number of individual investors, typically through the Internet, for a project or organization. *www.investorwords.com* Examples of crowdfunding sites are *www.kickstarter.com* and *www.gofundme.com*

Debt—A duty or obligation to pay money, deliver goods, or render service under an express or implied agreement. One who owes, is a debtor or debitor; one to whom it is owed, is a debtee, creditor, or lender.

Use of debt in an organization's financial structure creates financial leverage that can multiply yield on investment provided returns generated by debt exceed its cost. Because the interest paid on debt can be written off as an expense, debt is normally the cheapest type of long-term financing. *www.businessdictionary.com*

Debt [Reduction] Snowball Effect—The debt-snowball method is a debt reduction strategy, whereby one who owes on more than one account pays off the accounts starting with the smallest balances first, while paying the minimum payment on larger debts. Once the smallest debt is paid off, one proceeds to the next slightly larger small debt above that, so on and so forth, gradually proceeding to the larger ones later.[1] This method is sometimes contrasted with the debt stacking method, also called the "debt avalanche method", where one pays off accounts on the highest interest rate first. *en.wikipedia.org*

Delayed Gratification—Delayed gratification, or deferred gratification, is the ability to resist the temptation for an immediate reward and wait for a later reward. Generally, delayed gratification is associated with resisting a smaller but more immediate reward in order to receive a larger or more enduring reward later. *en.wikipedia.org*

Depreciating Asset—Accounting: The gradual conversion of the cost of a tangible capital asset or fixed asset into an operational expense (called depreciation expense) over the asset's estimated useful life. *www.businessdictionary.com*

Deregulation—Revision, reduction, or elimination of laws and regulations that hinder free competition in supply of goods and services, thus allowing market forces to drive the economy. *www.businessdictionary.com*

Differentiators—Unique features and/or benefits of a product, or aspects of a brand, that set it apart from competing products or brands. *www.businessdictionary.com*

Downline—Commission is earned on the agent's own sales revenue, as well as on the sales revenue of the sales-force recruited by the agent and his or her recruits (called downline). *www.businessdictionary.com*

Downsizing—Management: Intentional reduction in the size of a workforce at all staffing levels, to survive a downturn, improve efficiencies, or become a more attractive candidate for acquisition or merger. Used often as a euphemism for indiscriminately firing the employees. *www.businessdictionary.com*

Due Diligence—1. General: Measure of prudence, responsibility, and diligence that is expected from, and ordinarily exercised by, a reasonable and prudent person under the circumstances.

2. Business: Duty of a firm's directors and officers to act prudently in evaluating associated risks in all transactions. *www.businessdictionary.com*

"Elevator Pitch"—Very concise presentation of an idea covering all of its critical aspects, and delivered within a few seconds (the approximate duration of an elevator ride). *www.businessdictionary.com*

Emergency Fund—Money which is set aside for an emergency situation, such as unexpected unemployment or injury, or a natural disaster which destroys one's home and belongings. Having an emergency fund should be part of any individual or family's disaster plan. Emergency funds should be kept in a safe but easily accessible place, such as a savings account. The typical suggestion for an emergency fund is to have saved the equivalent of at least three months worth of living expenses. *www.businessdictionary.com*

Employment Contracts—Voluntary, deliberate, and legally enforceable (binding) agreement between an employer and an employee. Employment contracts can cover a variety of procedures and/or policies that the employee must agree to as a condition of his/her employment. Most employment contracts are required because the employer is seeking to protect its own interest. The contract may require that the employee not work for a competitor or even work in a similar industry during a designated time frame after they leave the company. *www.businessdictionary.com*

Entrepreneur—"'Someone who brings value to an idea.' I couldn't have said it any simpler or better. I believe entrepreneurs have a special knack for identifying problems that can be solved by their unique solution." *David Thomas Roberts, author of Unemployable!*

Someone who exercises initiative by organizing a venture to take benefit of an opportunity and, as the decision maker, decides what, how, and how much of a good or service will be produced. An entrepreneur supplies risk capital as a risk taker, and monitors and controls the business activities. The entrepreneur is usually a sole proprietor, a partner, or the one who owns the majority of shares in an incorporated venture. According to economist Joseph Alois Schumpeter (1883-1950), entrepreneurs are not necessarily motivated by profit but regard it as a standard for measuring achievement or success. Schumpeter discovered that they greatly value self-reliance, strive for distinction through excellence, are highly optimistic (otherwise nothing would be undertaken), and always favor challenges of medium risk (neither too easy, nor ruinous). *www.businessdictionary.com*

Entrepreneurship—The capacity and willingness to develop, organize and manage a business venture along with any of its risks in order to make a profit. The most obvious example of entrepreneurship is the starting of new businesses.

In economics, entrepreneurship combined with land, labor, natural resources and capital can produce profit. Entrepreneurial spirit is characterized by innovation and risk-taking, and is an essential part of a nation's ability to succeed in an ever changing and increasingly competitive global marketplace. *www.businessdictionary.com*

Equity—1. Ownership interest or claim of a holder of common stock (ordinary shares) and some types of preferred stock (preference shares) of a company. On a balance sheet, equity represents funds contributed by the owners (stockholders) plus retained earnings or minus the accumulated losses.

2. Net worth of a person or company computed by subtracting total liabilities from the total assets. In case of cooperatives, equity represents members' investment plus retained earnings or minus losses. *www.businessdictionary.com*

Exact Cash Position—The finite amount of liquid cash that is available to an individual measured on a daily basis.

Exit Strategy—Timing and means with which an investor (usually a venture capitalist [or the original entrepreneur]) cashes the investment in a startup venture or a buyout arrangement. It is often planned with, and agreed upon, by the management of the investee firm and commonly occurs after an initial public offering (IPO)[, sale or merger] of the startup. See also harvesting strategy. *www.businessdictionary.com*

Factoring [Accounts Receivable]—If a company needs to acquire cash quickly to maintain business operations, the company may sell off accounts receivable. By doing this, the company can gain an influx of cash to sustain through a financial crisis. *www.businessdictionary.com*

Failure—"Failure is never permanent; it's only a temporary obstacle to overcome. I don't know a single successful entrepreneur who hasn't experienced failures." *David Thomas Roberts, author of Unemployable!*

Family [Owned] Business—Company owned by one or more family members. In some cases, a family business may be owned by more than one family. *www.businessdictionary.com*

Features vs. Benefits—Selling a benefit or a solution that the customer wants or thinks is desirable as opposed to selling by feature.

Fiduciary Duty [Responsibility]—A legal obligation of one party to act in the best interest of another. The obligated party is typically a fiduciary, that is, someone entrusted with the care of money or property. Also called fiduciary obligation. *www.businessdictionary.com*

Financial Literacy—Possessing the knowledge necessary to understand concepts related to finance. These ideas may include balancing a checkbook, understanding interest rates, employee benefits, or how the stock market works. *www.investorwords.com*

Franchise—Commerce: (1) A privilege granted to make or market a good or service under a patented process or trademarked name. (2) A business operating under such privilege. *www.businessdictionary.com*

Franchise Memorandum and Agreement—A legal contract in which a well-established business consents to provide its brand, operational model and required support to another party for them to set up and run a similar business in exchange for a fee and some share of the income generated. The franchise agreement lays out the details of what duties each party needs to perform and what compensation they can expect. *www.businessdictionary.com*

Franchisee—One who purchases a franchise. The franchisee then runs that location of the purchased business. He or she is responsible for certain decisions, but many other decisions (such as the look, name, and products) are already determined by the franchisor and must be kept the same by the franchisee. The franchisee will pay the franchisor under the terms of the agreement, usually either a flat fee or a percentage of the revenues or profits, from the sales transacted at that location. *www.businessdictionary.com*

Franchisor—The company that allows an individual (known as the franchisee) to run a location of their business. The franchisor owns the overarching company, trademarks, and products, but gives the right to the franchisee to run the franchise location, in return for an agreed-upon fee. *www.businessdictionary.com*

Free Enterprise System—Business governed by the market forces of demand and supply, un-restrained by undue government interference through excessive controls and regulations. In general, a synonym for capitalism. *www.businessdictionary.com*

Future Profitability [Profit Potential]—The capacity for making more money in future transactions in business and trading. Profit potential is an important factor in any business or investment plan, and it is often a key element in the assessment of high percentage trades in the various asset markets. *www.businessdictionary.com*

Gig Economy—Refers to paying "gigs" or "projects" a person might get that are typically unrelated to each other by the same person. For example, someone might get a gig to play his or her guitar at a coffee shop three nights a week, but the same person may drive for Uber or take on various other projects or contract-only projects. Sometimes referred to as the "Uber Economy," it is the willingness to string many gigs together in order to make a living not encumbered by the traditional 8-5 job. It is a concept widely adopted by millennials.

Gross Revenues—The amount of money that the purchasers of a company's products and/or services actually pay for those items. Can also be referred to as raw sales income. *www.businessdictionary.com*

Growth Potential—Mathematical probability that a business will become larger. The growth potential refers to amount of sales or revenues the organization generates. *www.businessdictionary.com*

Income Streams—The flow of money generated by a business from different products or services. Can also refer to multiple streams of income from various sources.

Independent [Business] Valuation—The process of examining various economic factors of a business using predetermined formulas to assess the value of the business or an owner's interest in a company. Business valuation may be conducted to provide an accurate snapshot of the company's financial standing to present to current or potential investors. The Internal Revenue Service requires that a business be valued based on fair market value. *www.businessdictionary.com*

Initial Public Offering (IPO)—First offering of a firms' stock (shares) on the stockmarket, at the time it 'goes public.' Because a stockmarket usually values the stock on the expectations of the firm's future growth and income, IPOs are typically an opportunity for the founders and other early investors to make high profits by cashing their stockholdings. *www.businessdictionary.com*

Institutional Investors—Large organizations (such as banks, finance companies, insurance companies, labor union funds, mutual funds or unit trusts, pension funds) which have considerable cash reserves that need to be invested. Institutional investors are by far the biggest participants in securities trading and their share of stock market volumes have consistently grown over the years. For example, on a typical day, about 70 percent of the trading on the NYSE is on the behalf of institutional investors. Because they are considered knowledgeable and strong enough to safeguard their own interests, institutional investors are relatively less restricted by the security regulations designed to protect smaller investors. *www.businessdictionary.com*

Intellectual Property—Knowledge, creative ideas, or expressions of human mind that have commercial value and are protectable under copyright, patent, servicemark, trademark, or trade secret laws from imitation, infringement, and dilution. Intellectual property includes brand names, discoveries, formulas, inventions, knowledge, registered designs, software, and works of artistic, literary, or musical nature. It is one of the most readily tradable properties in the digital marketplace. *www.businessdictionary.com*

Job Description—A broad, general, and written statement of a specific job, based on the findings of a job analysis. It generally includes duties, purpose, responsibilities, scope, and working conditions of a job along with the job's title, and the name or designation of the person to whom the employee reports. Job description usually forms the basis of job specification. *www.businessdictionary.com*

Key Man Life Insurance Policy [Key Person Insurance]—Life and/ or disability insurance on one (or more) key persons whose loss or unavailability may cause loss of profit, goodwill, or increase in expenses. These insurance policies help finance the search and training of a successor, or compensate for fall in profits. Also called key employee insurance. *www.businessdictionary.com*

Liabilities—1. Finance: A claim against the assets, or legal obligations of a person or organization, arising out of past or current transactions or actions. Liabilities require mandatory transfer of assets, or provision of services, at specified dates or in determinable future.

2. Accounting: Accounts and wages payable, accrued rent and taxes, trade debt, and short and long-term loans. Owners' equity is also termed a liability because it is an obligation of the company to its owners. Liabilities are entered on the right-hand of the page in a double-entry bookkeeping system. *www.businessdictionary.com*

Liquidity Event—The way in which an investor plans to close out an investment[, wherein all parties involved (including the original founders or entrepreneur) cash in.] For example, a venture capitalist or angel investor may look to an IPO or acquisition as his/her exit strategy. also called exit strategy. *www.investorwords.com*

Loan Document—Document that records the loan agreement between a borrower and a lender. Also called loan document. *www.businessdictionary.com*

Market Share—A percentage of total sales volume in a market captured by a brand, product, or company. *www.businessdictionary.com*

Marketing Plan—Product specific, market specific, or company-wide plan that describes activities involved in achieving specific marketing objectives within a set timeframe. A market plan begins with the identification (through market research) of specific customer needs and how the firm intends to fulfill them while generating an acceptable level of return. It generally includes analysis of the current market situation (opportunities and trends) and detailed action programs, budgets, sales forecasts, strategies, and projected (proforma) financial statements. See also marketing strategy. *www.businessdictionary.com*

Mentor—A mentor is an individual, usually older, always more experienced, who helps and guides another individual's development. This guidance is not typically done for personal gain.

Micro Business—"A micro business is a business that is either part-time or has no more than two employees. According to the U.S. Census website, micro businesses make up 95 percent of the twenty-eight million businesses tracked by the federal government." *David Thomas Roberts, author of Unemployable!*

Millennials—"Those 18-35 years old at the writing of this book. Millennials have grasped the emergence of new technologies with a voracious appetite. Many millennials, like all entrepreneurs, openly question the status quo and why certain behaviors for business, life and society are the way they are." *David Thomas Roberts, author of Unemployable!*

Mutual Confidentiality and Non-Disclosure Document [Non-circumvention-non-disclosure-NCND-agreement]— Instrument used in early stages of a business transaction arranged by brokers (intermediaries). Its purpose is to ensure that (1) the intermediaries (who brought the buyer and seller together) are not by-passed and

(2) the information disclosed during the negotiations is not revealed to any external or unauthorized party. *www.businessdictionary.com*

National Consumption-Based Tax—A consumption tax is a tax on spending on goods and services. The tax base of such a tax is the money spent on consumption. *www.fairtax.org*

Nepotism—Practice of appointing relatives and friends in one's organization to positions for which outsiders might be better qualified. Despite its negative connotations, nepotism (if applied sensibly) is an important and positive practice in the startup and formative years of a firm where complete trust and willingness to work hard (for little or no immediate reward) are critical for its survival. *www.businessdictionary.com*

Net Profits—The amount by which income from sales is larger than all expenditure. Also called profit after tax. *www.businessdictionary.com*

Network Marketing—"(Network Marketing is a) Direct selling method in which independent agents serve as distributors of goods and services, and are encouraged to build and manage their own sales force by recruiting and training other independent agents. In this method, commission is earned on their own sales revenue, as well as on the sales revenue of the sales-force recruited by the agent and his or her recruits (called downline)." *www.businessdictionary.com*

Non-Compete Agreement—Provision in a business sale agreement that restricts the seller from starting or working in a similar business for a certain number of years (typically three) in a specified geographical area. *www.businessdictionary.com*

Non-Disclosure Agreement (NDA)—A contract that restricts the disclosure of confidential information or proprietary knowledge under specific circumstances. Non-disclosure agreements are often signed by companies discussing a potential partnership, or can be required by employers so that employees do not divulge confidential information about the company to non-employees. A non-disclosure agreement will usually contain very specific information, typically including exactly what type of information cannot be shared, and then exceptions for when this information is allowed to be shared. A non-disclosure agreement usually lasts for a pre-determined length of time, which is generally specified within the agreement. *www.investorwords.com*

Non-Performing Family Member—"A family member who is a bad employee is worse than an employee nobody is related to. Bad apples that are from the same tree have a propensity to infect the rest of the staff at an alarming rate. Recognize this in its earliest stages and make the tough decision to boot a non-performing family member. You might have family relationships to repair, but make sure family members understand that they are held to a higher standard." *David Thomas Roberts, author of Unemployable!*

Overhead Cost—Ongoing operational expenses incurred by a business. These expenses may be referred to as operational costs. Items such as utilities, rent, subscriptions are all examples of overhead expenses. *www.businessdictionary.com*

Partnership Agreement—Written agreement between two or more individuals who join as partners to form and carry on a for-profit business. Among other things, it states the (1) nature of the business, (2) capital contributed by each partner, and (3) their rights and responsibilities. A partnership does not have a separate legal existence like an incorporated firm, and the partners are jointly and severally liable for the debts of the firm. Even on withdrawing from the partnership they remain liable for already incurred debts, and for future debts unless a proper notice of retirement is published. A valid partnership, however, can exist without a written agreement in which case the provisions of the statutes governing partnerships would apply. Also called agreement of partnership. See also articles of partnership. *www.businessdictionary.com*

Payback Schedule—In an equity or debt investment, a written contract document is absolutely necessary. The document should state the terms of the deal, payback schedule (if debt), equity ownership (if applicable) and a definitive statement that the investors or loaners know they may lose their entire investment. *David Thomas Roberts, author of Unemployable!*

Perceived Value—A customer's opinion of a product's value to him or her. It may have little or nothing to do with the product's market price, and depends on the product's ability to satisfy his or her needs or requirements. *www.businessdictionary.com*

Percentage Ownership [Equity Stake]—The percentage of a business owned by the holder of some number of shares of stock in that company. Shareholders of a significant equity stake in a company may exercise some level of control, influence, or participation in the activities of the company. Acquisition of a sufficiently large equity stake in a company can also enable a company or individual to initiate a merger, buyout, or other transfer of ownership. *www.businessdictionary.com*

[Performance] Metrics—Standards of measurement by which efficiency, performance, progress, or quality of a plan, process, or product can be assessed. *www.businessdictionary.com*

Poor Man's Franchise—"Some call it a 'poor man's franchise.' Others ignorantly and erroneously refer to network marketing as a pyramid scheme." *David Thomas Roberts, author of Unemployable!*

Potential Liabilities—"There are fiduciary responsibilities and potential liabilities, including the likelihood of required annually audited financials (expensive), annual shareholders' meetings and a board of directors." *David Thomas Roberts, author of Unemployable!*

Private Equity [Groups]—Money invested in firms which have not 'gone public' and therefore are not listed on any stock exchange. Private equity is highly illiquid because sellers of private stocks (called private securities) must first locate willing buyers. Investors in private equity are generally compensated when: (1) the firm goes public, (2) it is sold or merges with another firm, or (3) it is recapitalized. *www.businessdictionary.com*

Private Offering Memorandum—"This is also called a Section 504(D) offering because it is covered in that particular section of Securities and Exchange Commission (SEC) regulations. This type of private offering of equity shares of your company requires professional assistance. Do not try to do this on your own." *David Thomas Roberts, author of Unemployable!*

Private Sector—The part of national economy made up of private enterprises. It includes the personal sector (households) and corporate sector (companies), and is responsible for allocating most of the resources within an economy. See also public sector. *www.businessdictionary.com*

Pro Forma (Future Estimate) Financials—Assumed, forecasted, or informal information presented in advance of the actual or formal information. The common objective of a pro forma document is to give a fair idea of the cash outlay for a shipment or an anticipated occurrence. Pro forma financial statements give an idea of how the actual statement will look if the underlying assumptions hold true. Latin for, according to form or for form's sake. *www.businessdictionary.com*

Profit and Loss Statement—An official quarterly or annual financial document published by a public company, showing earnings, expenses, and net profit. Net income is determined from this financial report by subtracting total expenses from total revenue. The profit and loss statement and the balance sheet are the two major financial reports that every public company publishes. The difference between this statement and the balance sheet deals with the periods of time that each one represents. The profit and loss statement shows transactions over a given period of time (usually quarterly or annually), whereas the balance sheet gives a snapshot holdings on a specific date. also called income statement or earnings report. *www.investorwords.com*

Progressive [Income] Tax—Income tax that takes a larger percentage of a larger income and a smaller percentage of a smaller income. For example, a tax on luxury cars. See also proportional tax and regressive tax. *www.businessdictionary.com*

Pyramid (Ponzi) Scheme—Chain-recruiting scam in which the main objective is to continuously bring in new members (euphemistically called sales representatives, independent representatives, or even 'investors') than to sell anything of real value. In this scheme, 'A' recruits 'B' and 'C,' who in turn recruit 'D' and 'E' and 'F' and 'G,' who in turn recruit ... and so on. Every new member pays an entrance fee (typically called 'investment' or some other beguiling name) which is divided among his or her recruiter, recruiter's recruiter, and ... right up to the originator of the scheme. This charade continues until the whole structure collapses from the ever growing need for more and more gullible recruits and everybody (except the promoters and the early recruiters) loses out. See also Ponzi scheme. Not to be confused with pyramiding. *www.businessdictionary.com*

Renegade Capitalist®—"A *Renegade Capitalist®* challenges the norms of traditional business models to fit his or her definition of what makes any particular business a success.

"*A Renegade Capitalist®* applies his or her unconventional ideas to capitalism, an economic system in which investment in and ownership of the means of production, distribution, and exchange of wealth is made and maintained chiefly by private individuals or corporations instead of government-owned means of wealth." *David Thomas Roberts, author of Unemployable!*

***Renegade Capitalist®* Quotient**—"The formula works like this: (Start-up Costs + Overhead + Effort) X Residual Factor/Time = *Renegade Capitalist®* Quotient." *David Thomas Roberts, author of Unemployable!*

Renegade Marketing®—The concept of marketing authored and developed by David Thomas Roberts that uses unconventional means not typically taught in business schools to identify, acquire and keep paying customers.

Residual Income—The concept of making a sale once and getting paid over and over again similar to a life insurance policy sold by an insurance agent.

Return on Investment (ROI)—The earning power of assets measured as the ratio of the net income (profit less depreciation) to the average capital employed (or equity capital) in a company or project. *www.businessdictionary.com*

Expressed usually as a percentage, return on investment is a measure of profitability that indicates whether or not a company is using its resources in an efficient manner. For example, if the long-term return on investment of a company is lower than its cost-of-capital, then the company will be better off by liquidating its assets and depositing the proceeds in a bank. Also called rate of return, or yield. *www.businessdictionary.com*

Right-To-Work State—[A state that has enacted] Legislation that allows a person to work at any place of employment without being forced to join a union as a condition of employment. *www.businessdictionary.com*

Risk-Aversion [Risk-Averse]—Risk-aversion is a preference for a sure outcome over a gamble with higher or equal expected value. *en.wikipedia.org*

Risk Management—The identification, analysis, assessment, control, and avoidance, minimization, or elimination of unacceptable risks. An organization may use risk assumption, risk avoidance, risk retention, risk transfer, or any other strategy (or combination of strategies) in proper management of future events. *www.businessdictionary.com*

Schedule C—A Schedule C is a tax form that owners of a small business file along with their 1040. Business owners use the form to report their income, expenditures and losses to the Internal Revenue Service. Independent contractors who work for companies but are not considered employees also use a Schedule C. *http://get.smarter.com*

Scheduled Monthly Close—"The disciplined entrepreneur has a scheduled monthly close of his or her books and a profit and loss statement to study... I insist on a hard close of my businesses monthly. This means we pick a date, close out the books for the month, produce a profit and loss statement, pay any taxes due, and make any necessary adjustments to improve the outlook for the next month." *David Thomas Roberts, author of Unemployable!*

Search Engine Optimization (SEO)—Refers to the process of improving traffic to a given website by increasing the site's visibility in search engine results. Websites improve search engine optimization by improving content, making sure that the pages are able to be indexed correctly, and ensuring that the content is unique. Going through the search engine optimization process typically leads to more traffic for the site because the site will appear higher in search results for information that pertains to the site's offerings. *www.businessdictionary.com*

Section 504(D) Offering—Rule 504 of Regulation D provides an exemption from the registration requirements of the federal securities laws for some companies when they offer and sell up to $1,000,000 of their securities in any 12-month period. Companies under this exemption do not have to file reports with the SEC, but come with certain restrictions not common with publicly-traded securities. *www.sec.gov*

Securities and Exchange Commission (SEC)—US federal agency established in 1934 to help protect investors by enforcing securities-related laws, and by setting mandatory standards for disclosure of financial and other pertinent information about firms whose securities are traded over a stock exchange. Its five commissioners (appointed by the US President and confirmed by the Senate) serve for staggered five-year terms, and at any time no more than three of them may be from the same political party. *www.businessdictionary.com*

Shareholders' Agreement and Formal Subscription Document—A document required by the SEC and certain state regulatory bodies that define the risks associated with investing in a Section 504(D) private memorandum offering. (Note there are special rules that may vary by state.) *www.sec.gov*

Shark Tank®—*Shark Tank*, the critically-acclaimed reality show that has reinvigorated entrepreneurship in America, has also become a culturally defining series. The Sharks — tough, self-made, multi-millionaire and billionaire tycoons — continue their search to invest in the best businesses and products that America has to offer. The Sharks will once again give people from all walks of life the chance to chase the American dream, and potentially secure business deals that could make them millionaires. *http://abc.go.com*

Social Media—Primarily internet or cellular phone based applications and tools to share information among people. Social media includes popular networking websites, like Facebook and Twitter; as well as bookmarking sites like Digg or Reddit. It involves blogging and forums and any aspect of an interactive presence which allows individuals ability to engage in conversations with one another, often as a discussion over a particular blog post, news article, or event. *www.businessdictionary.com*

Socialism—An economic system in which goods and services are provided through a central system of cooperative and/or government ownership rather than through competition and a free market system. *www.businessdictionary.com*

Sole Proprietor—Sole owner of a business; a self-employed person such as a grocer, plumber, or taxi driver. He or she directs the affairs of the enterprise, bears its risks and losses, and takes the profits and benefits. Also called sole trader. *www.businessdictionary.com*

Startups—Early stage in the life cycle of an enterprise where the entrepreneur moves from the idea stage to securing financing, laying down the basis structure of the business, and initiating operations or trading. *www.businessdictionary.com*

Success—"Success for me is the freedom to do the things I love without others controlling my time, income or schedule, and without worrying about money." *David Thomas Roberts, author of Unemployable!*

"Sweat" Equity—1. Increased worth of a business (over and above the money invested) created by the unpaid mental and/or physical hard work of the founder/owner. *www.businessdictionary.com*

Tax Deduction for Mortgage Interest—Generally, home mortgage interest is any interest you pay on a loan secured by your home (main home or a second home). The loan may be a mortgage to buy your home, a second mortgage, a line of credit, or a home equity loan. The IRS allows for deductions of this interest based on certain criteria. *www.irgs.gov*

Telecom Expense Management—Refers to the systems deployed by a business to process, pay, and audit corporate telecom expenses. Expense management includes the policies and procedures that govern such spending, as well as the technologies and services utilized to process and analyze the data associated with it.

Software to manage the expense claim, authorization, audit and repayment processes can be obtained from organizations that provide a licensed software, implementation and support service, or alternatively, from software as a service (SAAS) providers. SAAS providers offer on-demand web-based applications managed by a third party to improve the productivity of expense management.

Term Life Insurance—Simplest and usually the cheapest type of life insurance that stays in effect for a specified period or until a certain age of the insured. It pays the face amount of the policy in case the insured dies within the coverage period (term) but pays nothing if he or she outlives it. Also, (unlike in whole life insurance) whereas it premium cost is low in younger years, it generally increases rapidly with the age of the insured. Term life insurance is used commonly as an insurance cover for a loan repayment or post-death liabilities such as estate taxes. Also called term insurance. *www.businessdictionary.com*

"Termiting"—"Termiting your way through a customer means that you make sure you have relationships at every level throughout the account. This means everyone from the lowest level contact you have all the way to the C-suite." *David Thomas Roberts, author of Unemployable!*

Time Management—"The single most important skill for success for a sales entrepreneur. Time is truly money in this profession and everything else is secondary to being in front of qualified prospects on a daily basis." *David Thomas Roberts, author of Unemployable!*

Trade Secrets—Type of intellectual property such as formulary, know how, process, system, or confidential information that gives its owner a competitive advantage and unauthorized disclosure of which will harm the owner. Courts generally grant injunctions to prevent a threatened disclosure of a trade secret by the current or former employees because otherwise the relationship of trust between the employer and employee will be destroyed. The employer must, however, demonstrate that he or she actively safeguarded the trade secret and had informed the employees that it was to remain confidential. *www.businessdictionary.com*

Unsustainable Debt—An economic situation where the cost of debt maintenance is so great that incoming revenues are not sufficient to continue servicing the debt and sustain essential costs of living, or

in the case of a nation, to sustain essential services.
www.businessdictionary.com

Upfront Loading of Products/Services—"Front loading" occurs
when the new reps are required or financially incentivized to buy
an extraordinary amount of product upon enrolling. Legally, the
purchase of inventory must always be optional.
http://thompsonburton.com

Upline—In network marketing, those who have sponsored you into the
business and their uplines.

"Use of Funds" Strategy—"A clear 'use of funds' strategy is critical
to an investor and should not be used to fund the entrepreneur's
salary." *David Thomas Roberts, author of Unemployable!*

Value Add—[Creation] of a competitive advantage by bundling,
combining, or packaging features and benefits that result in greater
customer acceptance. *www.businessdictionary.com*

Variable Interest Rate—Interest rate that fluctuates over the term of a
loan on the basis of changes in an index that reflects changes in the
market rates of interest. *www.businessdictionary.com*

Venture Capital Firms—An investment company that invests its
shareholders' money in startups and other risky but potentially very
profitable ventures. *www.investorwords.com*

Vested Interest—2. Personal stake, or expectation of personal gain,
that underlies a strong commitment to maintain or influence an
action. *www.businessdictionary.com*

Wealth Redistribution—Central tenet of most modern economies
whereby a nation's wealth is channeled, from those who have more
to those below a certain income level, through taxes that pay for
welfare benefits. *www.businessdictionary.com*

Work Ethic—The belief that work has a moral benefit and an inherent
ability to strengthen character. *www.businessdictionary.com*